ATLANTIS
IN
AMERICA

By LEWIS SPENCE

Author of " The Problem of Atlantis,"
" The Gods of Mexico," " The Myths of
Mexico and Peru," " The Civilisation of
Ancient Mexico," "The Popol Vuh," etc.

GW00645433

THE BOOK TREE

SAN DIEGO, CALIFORNIA

Originally published 1925
Ernest Benn Limited
London

New material, updated photographs,
revisions and cover
©2002
The Book Tree
All rights reserved

ISBN 1-885395-97-3

Cover layout and design
Lee Berube

Printed on Acid-Free Paper
in the United States
by LightningSource, Inc.

Published by
The Book Tree
P O Box 16476
San Diego, CA 92176

We provide fascinating and educational products to help awaken the public to new ideas and
information that would not be available otherwise.
Call 1 (800) 700-8733 for our *FREE BOOK TREE CATALOG*.

INTRODUCTION

Atlantis is a legendary continent that is said to have disappeared very suddenly sometime in the ancient past. There are almost as many theories about the location of Atlantis as there are books that have been written about it. Despite these many theories, the location of Atlantis remains, at least up until today, a mystery. Each separate theory regarding its location is presented well, in most cases, and this book is no exception.

One reason this book is being made available again, however, is because of the recent discovery of the remains of an ancient city in the Atlantic Ocean. It was found in deep water on the ocean floor off the western coast of Cuba in late 2001, discovered by a group of Canadian researchers using, among other things, an underwater robot and modern sonar. Images recovered portray, in their estimation, a city that existed over 6000 years ago on the slope of a volcano. If true, this is the oldest city ever found, far older than neighboring Mayan cities in Central America and dating back fifteen centuries before the estimated building of the Great Pyramid in Egypt. It may have sunk so far due to the neighboring volcano or an immense cataclysm, but we must wait for more information, as of this writing, for confirmation.

What we know so far has many speculating that this could have been Atlantis, or at least part of it. The immense water depth at its current location suggests a cataclysmic end to this city. When it did exist above water it may have helped to form a land bridge between Cuba and the Yucatan Peninsula, where ancient Mayan cities such as Uxmal and Chichen Itza can still be found. Sonar and the underwater robot have located huge megaliths similar to those found at Stonehenge and on Easter Island. Photographs taken and converted from advanced sonar have Cuban and U.S. scientists believing that streets, buildings and pyramids exist in this location. "Signs and inscriptions" have also been found on some of the monuments and structures, but have so far not been deciphered. A joint underwater excavation should have occurred in mid 2002 by Cuba and the Canadian company involved.

It is time to read this book again, and explore the other evidence for Atlantis in America. Spence wrote many books on ancient civilizations and was one of the best researchers of his time. In this book he puts forth evidence that Atlantis was located in the Western hemisphere—in and around Central America. The Mayan culture, argues Spence, adopted and shared many of the cultural marvels of Atlantis, including its layout of cities, impressive architecture and massive pyramids.

Spence does an impressive job of detective work by comparing Indian myths from various lands including Peru, Brazil, Central America, North America, and the Atlantean story from the great philosopher, Plato. Many of the myths he covers duplicate themselves in various cultures, leading one to believe that they must have had a common source. That source, according to Spence, was Atlantis.

More interesting evidence is shown through mummification, and how the common practice and methods of mummification had appeared not only in Egypt, but also in Europe and America in ways that *pre-dated* Egypt (which most people don't know). The common source for such a method of mummification, once again, according to Spence, would have to be Atlantis. He devotes an entire chapter on this subject, which is fascinating to read.

There is also a chapter on Quetzalcoatl, the primary God of the Mayas. Spence presents evidence that Quetzalcoatl was in fact the first Toltec king—a king who had migrated to his ruling city, Tollan, from a place called Antilla (Atlantis). The Mayan legends contain many references to Antilla. Their language is full of words with the root, Atl (as in Atlantis), and many place names seem to have adopted the root as well. Someday we shall find more solid connections to the intriguing clues found within the pages of this book. That someday may be approaching faster than one thinks. Out of all the books on Atlantis, this is one that should not be missed.

Paul Tice

PREFACE

THAT time has for ever departed when a farrago of myths collected at random, interspersed with wild etymologies and buttressed by dogmatic assertions passed for a justification of the Atlantean hypothesis. The older protagonists of Atlantis were delightful, but it was as Madame D'Aulnoy and Perrot are delightful. Brasseur de Bourbourg, Le Plongeon and the rest enchanted us, they led us like little children through the mazes of a country of fascination which Maeterlinck might cudgel his fancy in vain to produce, and hard must be his heart and thankless his spirit who does not look back upon their fantasies with gratitude and affection. For the man who can transform history into a glittering fable is as much a poet as he who reverses the process and makes the divine shapes of myth act and live on the stage of human story.

But to-day, when everyone is something of an archæologist, when nearly every page of the world's story has been translated into the vulgar tongue, so to speak, in countless volumes which place the essence and synopsis of archæological effort within the reach of all, the wayfaring man is no longer to be beguiled. True, he values a good yarn as much as ever. But if it be an archæological yarn, it must be based on fact, for he will tell you that not only does he lack the leisure to listen to fairy tales, and that these, in the main, are unprofitable in a hard world, but that he has discovered that after all there is no such legend as the legend which turns out to be true, and that the whole grey-golden limbo of wonderland can produce no such wealth of marvel and miracle as the heights and depths, the hidden profundities and shadowy abysses of our own wonderful star.

In a manner I agree with him, for fairy gold is only too apt to turn to leaves, whereas the more ponderable marvels abide as a joy and a prodigy for ever. But is the materially marvellous different in kind from the spiritually remote ? I doubt it. In any case, the first holds elements of wonder more immediately satisfying to most of us. The gilded treasures of a long-lost Pharaoh, the epic of a world-flight, the elfin voices of wireless, the plunging reality of the ocean leviathans dredged up by Mr. Mitchell Hedges,

the actuality of those Isthmian savages who trembled at
the name of magic, discovered by Lady Richmond Brown,
the strange new dimensional phases and loops of Relativity,
the unplumbed ocean of the subconscious mind, the glandular Élixir of Youth, the invasion of the atom's integrity
—are these not as rare, as full of gramarye to the imagination as a whole ocean of Fortunate Isles peopled by syren
shadows ? Science is daily raising the morocco covers of
The Thousand and One Nights to an ever more inaccessible shelf in the dusty library of Lord Rosebery's dead
and forgotten books.

So it is both by predilection and under force of popular
opinion that I write of Atlantis in the plain language of
fact, assured that in the process I do not cast marvel
behind me, but merely enter a new and more spacious
satrapy of that wonderland, to gain which the dreary
deserts of common sense have had to be traversed by many
a hardy but patient pilgrim wandering from the beaten
track of erudition. So far as my judgment serves me, I
shall set down nothing in these pages of the illogical or
the far-fetched, but shall endeavour to proceed to my
conclusions by the paths of ascertained fact and rational
argument. Doubtless prejudices and prepossessions will
beset my way, and the value of my premises will be
denied by those of clearer vision, just as others may, by
virtue of a higher gift of dialectic, succeed in overturning
my general thesis, and rank me with Brasseur, Le Plongeon
and the rest of my predecessors in the Atlantean argument.

As that argument unfolds, the reader will discover that
it pivots upon what I call the Atlantis culture-complex.
I hold that the occurrence on either side of the Atlantic
of a civilisation having certain salient cultural characteristics proves that Europe and Africa on the one hand and
America on the other must have received it from a common
source—Atlantis. The chief components of this complex
are a common tradition of cataclysm, mummification,
witchcraft, and certain art-forms and distinctive customs. These have, as will be seen, many inter-relations,
and all of them appear to me to find a nucleus
in the symbol of the thunder-stone, the fetish of the
Atlantean and European Poseidon and the Mexican
Quetzalcoatl alike. Whether I am right or wrong in my

inferences, I believe it will still be granted that I have at least established the facts that such a culture-complex existed in both the Western Old World and the New, and that it did not exist in Asia, in its primal integrity at least, as the traces of it in that continent are few, vague and scattered. I hold, then, that the evidence justifies me in looking for the place of its original development in an Atlantic area midway between the regions where its most salient manifestations are to be found.

As this book deals mainly with the evidence for the survival of Atlantean civilisation in the American continent, I have, through considerations of space, been compelled somewhat to abridge the proof which deals with the larger question of the former existence of Atlantis itself. This proof I have already presented in *The Problem of Atlantis*, but the reader will find it carefully summarised in these pages, in which, however, it will be found that my chief object has been to demonstrate the existence of Atlantean culture on American soil and to compare its manifestations there with those shoots it put forth in Europe.

L. S.

Edinburgh, *May*, 1925.

Plate I.—MAYA-TOLTEC TYPE OF ARCHITECTURE AT CHICHEN-ITZA, YUCATAN

CONTENTS

LIST OF PLATES

ILLUSTRATIONS IN THE TEXT

Atlantis in America

CHAPTER I

ATLANTIS AND ANTILLIA

THE tradition that the Atlantic Ocean holds in its depths the wreck of a great island-continent which once boasted a flourishing civilisation is deeply rooted in the minds of thousands. No amount of scientific protestation seems capable of shaking the world-wide conviction in the former existence of Atlantis. I hold this belief to be a natural and almost instinctive one, but I do not regard so favourably the widespread notion that Atlantis was the mother of all civilisation. Such an attitude is, of course, quite as unscientific as that which regards Egypt as the *fons et origo* of all culture. Culture must undoubtedly have had its birthplace in some one region of the earth's surface. But to infer from such an obvious fact that the entire apparatus of civilisation was evolved from an Atlantean, Egyptian or any other single source is wilfully to close one's eyes to those special and separate manifestations of it which arise out of the necessities of environment.

When I say, therefore, that I believe civilisation was carried to Europe from the now sunken continent of Atlantis, I must be understood as implying not that all civilisation, but a certain type of it alone was brought to early Europe from Atlantis. The Atlantean hypothesis will gain nothing by being pushed to extremes, or from the attentions of cranks. If it is worth examining at all, it is worth examining sanely.

Did the Atlantean type of culture succeed in reaching the shores of America as well as those of Europe in early times? I believe that it did. But I cannot credit the statements of some enthusiastic antiquaries that it reached American soil thousands of years prior to the Christian era. If a prolonged study of the conditions of civilisation in pre-Columbian America has made one thing more clear to me than another, it is that the culture of the Maya people of Central America, which was probably the most venerable on American soil, cannot be assigned to an antiquity in the region of its earliest settlement there greater than the second century prior to the Christian era.

To substantiate such a theory as that which relates to the penetration of Atlantean culture to the American continent is naturally a matter of surpassing difficulty. In the first place, we are dealing with a culture no ponderable or material monuments or relics of which remain. Again and again we must have recourse to analogy and assumption. A whole literature, remarkable for its interest, erudition and ingenuity has crystallised round the subject. Much of it has been condemned, and with reason, as the fantastic outpourings of erudite irresponsibles. On the other hand, those who have criticised the hypothesis most unmercifully have too often evinced that credulity of incredulity which has left its mark so indelibly on Victorian science.

In these pages I have endeavoured to collect the proofs and evidences of the theory that from the now submerged Atlantic land-mass which is known both to tradition and geology as Atlantis the beginnings of a certain type of culture were conveyed to American as well as to European soil. In the present state of our knowledge the precise value of the cultural debt which pre-Columbian America owed to Atlantis cannot well be estimated. But it is surely needless to say that the belief in such a transference would scarcely commend itself to any rational mind unless very obvious and striking evidential material already existed to compel attention to it. Such material exists, but our knowledge of aboriginal American civilisation is presently so imperfect that we can only grope our way rather painfully by the light of a few well-ascertained facts through a gloaming of probabilities, where much of the scenery is a little unreal. But as our vision grows more accustomed to the twilight of this obscure atmosphere, the shapes of things discerned take on a sharper outline, and in due time, perhaps, may be fully revealed to us.

The tradition of Atlantis has become part of the world's literature. Our first authentic notice of it is to be found in the writings of Plato, who in his *Timæus* preserves a tale told by a certain Critias to Timæus and Socrates, based on writings and traditions which Dropidas, the great-grandfather of Critias, had handed down. This information Dropidas had received from Solon, who on his part had it at first hand from an Egyptian priest of Sais, about 600 B.C. Atlantis, said this hierophant, was a great continent situated in the Atlantic Ocean, over against the Strait of Gibraltar. About 9000 years before his time (9600 B.C.) its people swarmed into the Mediterranean area and invaded Greece. The Athenians attacked and defeated them, and were saved from further invasion by the sudden disappearance beneath the sea of the land whence their enemies had emerged. This catastrophe, it would appear from the context, was brought upon Atlantis by the will of the gods, whom its inhabitants had offended by their wickedness. All that remained of Atlantis in Plato's time were vast mud-banks, which made it difficult for vessels to negotiate the passage from the Mediterranean into the Atlantic.

At first sight the account of Plato has all the appearance of a legendary tale. But a careful examination of its text furnishes data for a reasonable case in favour of its authenticity. Again, practically all geological authorities are in agreement that such a continent once actually existed, and that the Canary Islands, the Azores and the Cape Verde Islands are the last vestiges of this land-mass. They also agree that it slowly disintegrated during a period of many thousands of years. The point on which they are chiefly at issue is that which has reference to the probable date of the final disappearance of its main portion.

The chief modern protagonists of the theory that Atlantis existed at a period in geological time when it was possible for it to have supported human life are Professor R. F. Scharff of Dublin and M. Pierre Termier, Director of Science of the Geological Chart of France. These authorities affirm that it is by no means improbable that such a continent as Plato described continued to exist in the Atlantic area until some nine or ten thousand years prior to the Christian era. They bring to bear upon the question a mass of corroborative evidence which is as staggering as it is ingeniously employed and arranged. Evidence from plant and animal life in the Atlantic islands is adduced to demonstrate the long isolation and development of the fauna and flora of these archipelagoes, and in some cases their European or American origin. These forms, it is believed, reached the islands via land-bridges which stretched on either hand to the European and American continents. The deep-sea soundings made by expeditions sent out by various European Governments undoubtedly assist the argument that the remains of sunken Atlantis occupy some portions of the bed of the Atlantic at no very great depths from its surface.[1]

As regards the existence of man on this Atlantic continent, now submerged, I believe the successive races which appeared in the Biscayan and Pyrenean regions of Spain and France during what is known as the Aurignacian and Azilian Periods of the Palæolithic Age (Old Stone Age) to have been immigrants from the slowly disintegrating continent of Atlantis. The first of these was the Crô-Magnon race, which arrived in Europe about 25,000 years ago. This was a tall people with large brain-case, possessing a stone culture and highly developed art which is known as Aurignacian, and was manifested in stone, bone and painting. Its beginnings cannot be traced anywhere in the known world. This race was succeeded about 14,000 B.C. by a second wave of similar type, whose art, known as Magdalenian, was more highly developed, and likewise has no known origin. A third race of immigrants, the Azilian-Tardenoisian, who arrived in Europe about 10,000 B.C., were the ancestors of the Iberian peoples, and no satisfactory origin has so far been accredited to them.

An important point for students of the Atlantis theory is that the Crô-Magnon remains show them to have been a people practically identical with the Guanche race which formerly peopled the Canary Islands, the last existing remnants of the sunken continent. The Guanches were isolated for countless centuries from Europe before their discovery by the Spaniards. Their customs and art, carving and cave-painting are practically identical, say Professor Osborn, Dr. Réné Verneau and the late Lord Abercromby, with those of the Crô-Magnons. The latter, at the epoch of their first arrival in Europe, were certainly without the means of navigation, and must have arrived

[1] Further evidence in favour of the former existence of an Atlantean continent will be found in Chapter II.

on European soil by means of a land-bridge. Nor were boats or ships yet invented at the era when they might have reached the Canaries by sea.[1]

In a former work I arrived at the following conclusions, based on the geological proof for the existence of Atlantis at a period approximate to that mentioned by Plato :

(1) That a great continent formerly occupied the whole or major portion of the North Atlantic region, and a considerable portion of its southern basin. Of early geological origin, it must, in the course of successive ages, have experienced many changes in contour and mass, probably undergoing frequent submergence and emergence.

(2) That in Miocene (Late Tertiary) times it still retained its continental character, but towards the end of that period it began to disintegrate, owing to successive volcanic and other causes.

(3) That this disintegration resulted in the formation of greater and lesser insular masses. Two of these, considerably larger in area than any of the others, were situated (a) at a relatively short distance from the entrance to the Mediterranean ; and (b) in the region of the present West India Islands. These may respectively be called Atlantis and Antillia. Communication was possible between them by an insular chain.

(4) That these two island-continents and the connecting chain of islands persisted until late Pleistocene times, at which epoch (about 25,000 years ago, or the beginning of the Post-Glacial epoch) Atlantis seems to have experienced further disintegration. Final disaster appears to have overtaken Atlantis about 10,000 B.C. Antillia, on the other hand, seems to have survived until a much more recent period, and still persists fragmentally in the Antillean[2] group, or West India Islands.

It would seem then that if Atlantean culture reached America it must have done so by way of the Antillian continent. Believing these conclusions to be well founded, I shall attempt to prove :

[1] Further proof of the identification of the Guanches with the Crô-Magnon race will be found in Chapter II.

[2] Throughout I employ the adjective " Antillean " to describe the Antilles or West India Islands, and " Antillian " to designate the continent of Antillia.

(1) That an ancient tradition referring to Antillia, and similar to that of Atlantis, formerly received widespread credence.

(2) That the Antilles are the remains of the ancient continent of Antillia.

(3) That this continent formerly had terrestrial and cultural connections with Atlantis.

(4) That it was the stepping-stone by which Atlantean culture reached the American mainland.

(1) That an ancient tradition referring to Antillia and similar to that of Atlantis, had formerly widespread credence !

References to the continent or island of Antillia are found in the maps, globes and geographical works of the pre-Columbian Period. These are so numerous and important as to give the impression that something more tangible than tradition lay behind them. It is essential to our proof to review these references and to see how far they justify such a tradition or belief.

One of the most striking of them is the reference to Antillia in a letter of Toscanelli to Columbus, dated 1474.[1] In this letter Toscanelli recommends the island of Antillia as a convenient half-way house on the voyage to Cathay. Behaim, on his globe of 1492, wrote under the outline of Antillia : " In 1414 a ship from Spain came nearest to it without danger." On the map of Ruysch (1508) it is stated that Antillia was discovered by the Spaniards " long ago," and he refers to the legend that King Roderick, the last of the Gothic kings of Spain, flying from the Moors, found an asylum in the eighth century.

Both globe and map depict Antillia as lying far west in the Atlantic, and quite apart from any other land, but in Peter Martyr's *Decades of the New World or West Indies* (*ca.* 1510) we find Antillia explicitly described as a well-known archipelago. At that period confusion existed between the West India Islands (the present Antilles) and Antillia, which certainly suggests that for generations Antillia had been traditionally recognised as an island-continent, and that the idea that the Antilles or West

[1] See Harisse, *Bibliotheca Americana Vetustissima*, XVI–XVIII.

India Islands were the remains of such a continent had not yet become general.

Still there were signs that such an idea was gaining ground. Nicolo de Canerio's map (1502 ?) describes the West India Islands as " Antilhas del Rey de Castilla," and an anonymous map of about the same date gives them the collective name of " Antilie."

But the tradition that Antillia was indeed a continent finds justification from other quarters. Long after the South American coast had been sufficiently explored to demonstrate its existence as a continental area it was identified with Antillia, as two maps in the Egerton MS.[1] distinctly prove. Here the name Antiglia is given to the mainland.

Later still, however, the conviction grew that the site of the true Antillia was that of the groups of islands since known as the Antilles, and this, I venture to suggest, proves almost conclusively that tradition, as is her wont, unerringly fixed upon a correct location. Scores of instances of this instinctive but nevertheless precise fixation of locality by tradition are known to every working student of folklore. Explorers in the realms of traditional lore, indeed, are becoming more and more accustomed to look for the horizon of actual sites in formerly discredited rural legends. And if this traditional memory be successfully applied to the discovery of the sites of buried cities and buildings, may it not also be employed with equal reason in the case of sunken continents ?

Certain writers have proclaimed their belief in the original unity of the names Antillia and Atlantis, and have held that the elongated quadrilateral shape of Antillia on ancient maps resembled that of Atlantis as described by Plato. But Humboldt pointed out that Plato ascribed this form to a particular district in Atlantis and not to the island-continent as a whole.[2] He believed the name to be derived from the Arabic Al-tin, signifying " the dragon." The Arabs were certainly among the early navigators of the Atlantic, and more than one Arabic romance places a dragon-like monster on a desolate Atlantic isle. But the reputation of Antillia as the sup-

---

[1] 2803 in the British Museum list.
[2] *Examen critique de l'histoire de la geographic du nouveau continent*, Vol. I, p. 193.

posed asylum of a Christian monarch is perhaps sufficient to discredit this etymology. The two old Portuguese words *ante* and *illa* (pronounced illia), that is " the opposite island," the island opposing the Portuguese coast, seem to provide a natural interpretation.

But a large group of islands roughly corresponding to the West Indies is found on the fifteenth-century maps of

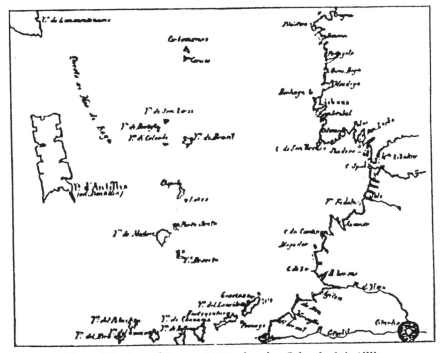

Map of Andreas Bianco, 1436, showing Island of Antillia.

Beccario, Bianco, Pareto, Roselli and Benincasa, all of which antedate the discovery of America. In Beccario's map of 1435 Antillia is clearly marked, and extends on the American side from the latitude of Morocco, a little south of the Strait of Gibraltar, to that of Northern Portugal. The last instance of a map in which the name Antillia is preserved is the Laon globe of 1493, the year succeeding the discovery. Mr. W. H. Babcock, a distinguished authority, identifies Antillia with the Antilles, and more especially with Cuba.[1]

[1] *Legendary Islands of the Atlantic*, p. 144 ff.

Sufficient proof has, I venture to think, been adduced to show that an ancient tradition referring to an Antillian continent had formerly widespread credence in Europe and North-western Africa before the time of Columbus. The natural inference is that it could only have found its way to these regions via Atlantis, and during the era prior to the submergence of that continent.

We may now pass on to a consideration of the question that the Antilles are the remains of the ancient continent of Antillia. This makes it necessary to examine the geological evidence for the possible former existence of an Antillian continent. [1]

Professor E. Suess in his *Antilitz der Erde* regards North and South America as two essentially distinct land-masses, and classifies the area of Central America and the Antilles as a third and entirely separate quantity. [2] "Almost everyone," says Scharff, "who has dealt with the flora and fauna of the West India Islands expresses his surprise at this fact." [3] An important point is the absence in the West Indies of the higher vertebrates in any appreciable number, and that although the soil and climate are most favourable to their presence in these islands. Thus Cuba has not half a dozen land mammals. This implies that the islands have not been connected with the mainland since early Tertiary times, or that their fauna must have been almost obliterated subsequently to its insular isolation. That fauna, such as it is, is markedly dissimilar to those of North and South America. But if its higher levels be impoverished, its humbler divisions are almost embarrassingly numerous, and we find in especial that its molluscs

---

[1] In order that the non-scientific reader may better be able to follow the evidence placed before him in this chapter, I have here appended a brief and simple outline of geological time :

PRIMARY OR PALÆOZOIC PERIOD—(Earliest forms of life).

SECONDARY OR MESOZOIC PERIOD—(Reptilia, birds).

TERTIARY PERIOD—Early Tertiary, divided into : Palæocene (mammals); Eocene (higher mammals) ; and Oligocene (Anthropoids). Late Tertiary, divided into : Miocene ; and Pliocene (Man).

QUATERNARY PERIOD—Pleistocene or Ice Age, divided into : Glacial and Post-Glacial. The beginning of the Pleistocene Age is, for practical purposes, generally reckoned at about 500,000 years ago. It is only in the last 25,000 years of this period that any form approaching modern man is to be found in Europe. The second division of the Quaternary is the Holocene, or "recent."

[2] P. 700.   [3] *Distribution and Origin of Life in America*, p. 261.

are capable of throwing much light on the whole question of how life made its way to the West India Islands.

If we cast a glance at any trustworthy map of the Antilles we observe at once that they are divided into two distinct groups, the Greater (Cuba, Haiti, Jamaica and Porto Rico) lying from west to east, and the Lesser (Guadeloupe, Dominica, Martinique, Barbadoes and the rest) extending in a semicircle from north to south. Suess believes the mountain system of the Greater Antilles to be merely a continuation of those of Yucatan and Guatemala, and the Greater Antilles as a whole are known to be composed of sedimentary rocks of the Mesozoic and First Tertiary Periods. On the other hand, the Lesser Antilles appear to be of recent and volcanic origin.

Professor R. T. Hill believes the Lesser Antilles to be the remains of an early isthmus connecting the North and South American continents, but there is certainly little or no faunistic evidence to support such a theory. He thinks that during part of the Eocene and Oligocene epochs of the Tertiary Period extensive subsidences submerged the Antilles, so that only the higher summits of Cuba, Haiti and Jamaica remained above water as small insular peaks. The West India Islands were later raised into one connected continental mass, which once more suffered gradual dismemberment, but at a still later period a second elevation took place, which, however, did not suffice to establish a united Antillean continent once again. Schuchert seems to be of the opinion that after a submergence in the Oligocene epoch all the islands disappeared, and that subsequently the Greater Antilles took their present shape. There thus seems to be a general consensus of opinion that at some time in the earlier part of the Tertiary era practically the whole of the Antillean area underwent a profound subsidence.

"The facts adduced by Dr. Simpson," says Scharff, "that the operculate species form so large a proportion of the Antillean land-snail fauna, that a majority of the genera is found on two or more of the islands and the mainland, while nearly every species is restricted to a single island, is a strong testimony to a former general land connection in this area. Dr. Simpson very carefully compared the molluscan fauna of the various islands with

one another and with that of the mainland, and bases his
conception of the geological history of the Antilles mainly
on the results so derived. He believes a considerable
portion of the species inhabiting the Greater Antilles to
be ancient, and to have developed on the islands where
they are now found. Probably at some time during the
Eocene Period the Greater Antilles were at a higher level,
so that the islands were united with one another and with
Central America. This resulted in an exchange of species
between the two regions. A land connection is also indicated between Cuba, the Bahamas and Florida. At this
time he thinks that the more northern isles of the Lesser
Antilles were not yet elevated above the sea, or, if so, they
have since probably been submerged. After this period
of elevation there followed one of general subsidence.
During it Jamaica was the first island to be separated,
then followed Cuba, and afterwards Haiti and Porto Rico.
The connection between the Antilles and the mainland
was broken, while the subsidence continued until only the
summits of the mountains of the four greater Antillean
islands remained above water. Eventually there was
another period of elevation which lasted, no doubt, until
the present time. The Bahamas gradually emerged and
were populated by forms drifted from Cuba and Haiti."[1]

Moreover, it has been proved that the centre of distribution of the Urocoptidæ, a family of small snails with a
fusiform shell, lies in the West Indies. Dr. Pilsbry in his
Manual of Conchology gives it as his opinion that there is
but scanty evidence of any direct land connection between
the Greater Antilles and the mainland of Central America
during the Tertiary Period. His researches confirm his
view and that of many geologists that originally there
was a large area of land of which the Antilles were the last
remnants, and that at some time during the Tertiary era
almost the whole of this ancient land was submerged,
gradually regaining its continental state.[2]

The close affinity between European and West Indian
molluscs has been remarked upon by several naturalists.
One carnivorous snail in especial, the Glandina, which has
its headquarters in the Antilles, is also found in the Medi-

---

[1] Op. cit., pp. 265-6.
[2] *Manual of Conchology*, XVI, pp. xx-xxiv.

terranean. It is impossible to regard it as a newcomer to
Europe, as it can be traced in disconnected patches
between the Caucasus and Algeria. Two other varieties
of molluscs found in the Mediterranean area, Leonia and
Tudorella, are also related to West Indian forms. This,
along with other considerations, has led Dr. Kobelt to the
conclusion that a land connection between the Antilles and
Europe persisted until Miocene times, and Boettger and
Andreae support the same theory.

The relationship of the animals of the Antilles has been
investigated by Scharff, who believes them to consist of
an admixture of exceedingly ancient with much more
modern types. All of them are distinct enough from the
forms of life on the mainland to make it certain, he thinks,
that the Greater Antilles had no recent land connection
either with Central America or the two neighbouring sub-
continents. The most ancient mammal found in the
West Indies is the curious snouted insect-eating Solenodon,
whose nearest relatives are the Centetidæ of Madagascar
and West Africa. It has two forms in the Antilles, the
Solenodon paradoxus, confined to Haiti, and the *Solenodon
cubanus*, native to Cuba. These differ somewhat in size,
colour and shape of skull, and thus constitute distinct
species. Professor Leche believes them to have passed by
a land-bridge from Madagascar to Brazil or the West Indies.

Two varieties of hutia, a rat-like rodent, are also entirely
confined to the West Indies, and Mr. Scharff thinks they
may have a remote Patagonian origin. There are in
Venezuela forms of this animal which might lead us to
think that it had gained admittance to the Antilles by an
old land-bridge across the Lesser Antilles. But no traces
of such a mammal exist there, and as a species of hutia is
found on Swan Island, it seems likely that the ancestors
of these animals reached the West Indies directly from
some western region.

"The main conclusion," writes Professor Scharff,
"which this brief study of the mammalian fauna of the
Antilles has revealed, is that the larger islands were formerly
united with one another, and with the Bahamas by land.
How far eastward this land extended cannot be determined
by the mammals, but it certainly must have reached
beyond the Virgin Islands to Anguilla, one of the most

northerly islands of the Lesser Antilles. Many islands of
the Lesser Antilles may have been completely submerged
at that time. Later on, Cuba, the Bahamas and Jamaica
were connected with the mainland after the other islands
had already been separated from the Antillean land-
mass, and lastly, Cuba and Jamaica were independently
joined to Central America before the existing physical
features were brought about."[1]

In his work on *Mexican Amphibians and Reptiles*
(pp. 234-7) Dr. H. Gadow concluded from a comparison of
the evidence from natural history and geology that the
Antilles had not been directly connected with the main
continent of North America since the Cretaceous Period.
Antillia, he believes, had only one continental connection,
namely, during the Miocene Period, and that by way of
Central America. This would make the whole of the flora
and fauna of the Antilles of Miocene origin at the least.

The Antilles seem to be little influenced by accidental
introductions. This is shown by the fact that few North
American butterflies, dragon-flies and moths are found
there, the great majority of these being Central American.
As regards the birds of the Antilles, Dr. Chapman makes
the suggestive statement that if it could be shown that
Central America was cut off from both continents at the
time when it was joined to the West Indies, the origin of
the insular fauna could be explained in a satisfactory
manner.

Dr. Ortmann is of the opinion that Central America,
the West Indies and the northern margin of South America
formed in the Mesozoic Period and certainly during the
Jurassic and Cretaceous Periods, a continental mass, the
Antillean continent, which was bounded by the sea on the
north and south. This continent broke up at the end of
the Cretaceous, the chief factor in its destruction being the
Caribbean Sea. The northern remnant of this mass,
consisting of the Greater Antilles and parts of the present
Central America, probably remained a unit up to the
Eocene Period. At the conclusion of the Eocene, he thinks,
and during the Oligocene and Miocene Periods, the connection between the Greater Antilles and the mainland
was severed, being subsequently re-established toward

[1] *Origin of Life in America*, pp. 286-7.

the end of the Tertiary era, and again destroyed in recent times.[1]

Criticising this statement, Scharff gives it as his opinion that in Cretaceous times South America was submerged and could not have formed part of an Antillean continent. " Towards the end of the Cretaceous Period all the Antilles except the Bahamas, were entirely covered by the sea, according to Professor Schuchert's maps. Yet, although the Peninsula of Yucatan was then submerged, no deposits of this age are known from Guatemala or Honduras, nor have any Mesozoic or Tertiary beds been discovered in those countries. . . . Possibly the Greater Antilles were not so completely covered by sea as is assumed. They may have been represented by small islands, and these would have possessed fragments of an ancient fauna and flora. . . . Some time during the Oligocene Period, Professor Schuchert again records a complete submergence of all the West Indian islands except the Bahamas. . . . A much more probable explanation is that the Antilles were reduced to small islands, and retained their own animals and plants. In early Miocene times all the Greater Antilles were certainly raised above the sea, and must have been then connected with one another. Jamaica was joined to Guatemala and Cuba to Mexico, but Jamaica must have been separated early from Haiti. While the islands were joined to one another, an intermingling of the more active ancient types occurred, the less progressive ones being forced to the higher altitudes by the new arrivals from Mexico and Central America. During the whole of Miocene times Yucatan was apparently below sea-level. When it rose in the Pliocene Period, it may have had a short land connection with the Antilles by way of Western Cuba. . . . Central America, during the existence of this Yucatan land-bridge, may still have been separated from North and South America. At this time the Lesser Antilles probably had an independent land connection with Venezuela ; but that there was an Antillean continent connected with the mainland in Pleistocene times, as suggested by Dr. Spencer, when Central America had already been invaded by the North and South American

[1] *Distribution of Freshwater Decapods*, p. 344 ff.

immigrants, is entirely opposed to the results derived from
a study of the fauna and flora."

Elsewhere in his most interesting work Professor
Scharff remarks on the subject of an Antillean continent :
" Central America and the Antilles, which are collectively
spoken of sometimes as the remnants of an ancient
' Antillean Continent,' possess a distinct and peculiar
fauna quite apart from the South American one which
has invaded this area. Towards the end of the Mesozoic
Period parts of this Antillean continent must have begun
to subside. About that time signs of the coming volcanic
activity appeared all along the Central American region.
During the successive igneous eruptions in early Tertiary
times, which have been continued with varied intensity to
the present day, the Atlantic Ocean seems to have invaded
the existing area of Central America and submerged
portions of it. . . . The movement of species seems to
have taken place from the West Indian area towards the
Pacific Ocean, thus implying the existence of a strong
current in that direction. Speaking of the Tertiary deposits of Tehuantepec, Dr. Böse remarks that the main mass
of the species contained therein are related to Atlantic
forms. Only very few show affinities with Pacific types.
Similar views were expressed by Professor Jordan and Dr.
Ortmann in regard to the recent marine fauna."

To sum up : Suess believes that North and South
America were formerly two different land-masses, and he
classes the Antilles and Central America as a third and
separate land-mass. In the Antilles there is an absence
of the higher vertebrates in any appreciable numbers.
This would seem to imply that the Antilles have not been
connected with the mainland since early Tertiary times.
The distribution of their mollusca seems to show, according to Scharff and others, that a land connection existed
between the Antilles and Europe until Miocene times.
Hill believes the Antilles were submerged during the
Eocene and Oligocene Periods, and that only their summits
remained above water. They were later raised into a
connected continental mass, which was once more dismembered, but at a later period still a second elevation
took place, which, however, failed to unite them entirely.
Schuchert thinks that after an Oligocene submergence the

Antilles disappeared, and that later the Greater Antilles took their present form. The consensus of opinion is that at some time in the Early Tertiary era practically the whole of the Antillean area underwent subsidence. The fact that certain genera of molluscs are found on certain of the islands and on the mainland, while nearly every species is restricted to a single island is strong testimony of a former general land connection in the Antillean area, and from this Simpson argues that during the Eocene Period the Greater Antilles were united with each other and with Central America, but underwent several alternate subsidences and elevations. Pilsbry thinks there is but scanty evidence for any direct land connection between the Antilles and the mainland during the Tertiary Period. He believes that there was formerly a large area of land, of which the Antilles are the last remnants, and that during the Tertiary era this land was submerged, later gradually regaining its continental position.

Scharff thinks the Antillean mammalia distinct enough from mainland forms to exclude the idea of recent land connections with the mainland. His main conclusion is that the Antilles were formerly united with one another and with the Bahamas, the Antillean continent stretching beyond the Virgin Islands to Anguilla. Later Cuba, the Bahamas and Jamaica were connected with the mainland after the other islands had already been separated from the Antillean land-mass, and Cuba and Jamaica were independently joined to Central America before the present disposition of land and water obtained.

Gadow believes in a continental connection during the Miocene. Ortmann is of opinion that Central America and the Antilles formed a continental mass during the Mesozoic Period, but that it broke up at the end of the Cretaceous, its northern remnant remaining a unit up to the Eocene. Land connection with the mainland was, however, re-established towards the end of the Tertiary Period, and destroyed in recent times only. Scharff, criticising these statements, believes that all the Greater Antilles were raised above the sea during the Miocene, and were then connected with each other. That, as suggested by Spencer, there was an Antillean continent connected with the mainland in Pleistocene times, he thinks improbable. Towards the end of the Mesozoic Period parts of the Antillean continent must have begun to subside. Movements of species seem to have taken place from the Antillean area towards the Pacific Ocean, thus implying the existence of a strong current in that direction.

From the consensus of geological opinion we seem therefore to be justified in saying that an Antillean continent formerly existed. The general view seems to be that it was partially submerged in Tertiary times, later rising to its present position as an archipelago. But there is plenty of good evidence that it retained its continental form until a relatively late date, and to this I prefer to adhere. I also believe that it had intercourse with Atlantis long before the disappearance of the latter continent, and that its people drew the seeds of their culture therefrom.

This brings us to the third of our propositions : That Antillia formerly had terrestrial and cultural relations with Atlantis, which must form the subject of another chapter.

CHAPTER II

THE CRÔ-MAGNONS OF AMERICA

IN approaching our third proposition that Antillia had a terrestrial and cultural connection with Atlantis at a period prior to the submergence of the last vestiges of that continent, we find that it naturally divides itself into two heads : (a) that which requires proof of a terrestrial connection, and (b) that which demands evidence of a cultural connection.

As regards its terrestrial connection with Atlantis, it will be necessary briefly to retrace our steps for a moment, and review the evidence in favour of the possible existence of a great continent of which both Atlantis and Antillia were the last remaining fragments.

M. Termier, whom we have already quoted, believes that " a North Atlantic continent comprising Russia, Scandinavia, Great Britain, Greenland and Canada, to which was added later a southern band made up of a large part of Central and Western Europe and an immense portion of the United States " formerly existed. " There was also," he says, " a South Atlantic, or African-Brazilian continent, extending northward to the southern border of the Atlas, eastward to the Persian Gulf and Mozambique Channel, westward to the eastern border of the Andes, and to the sierras of Colombia and Venezuela. Between the two continents passed the Mediterranean depression, that ancient maritime furrow which has formed an escarp about the earth since the beginning of geologic time, and which we see so deeply marked in the present Mediterranean, the Caribbean Sea and the Sunda or Flores Sea. A chain of mountains broader than the chain of the Alps, and perhaps in some parts as high as the majestic Himalayas, once lifted itself on the land-enclosed shore of the North Atlantic continent, embracing the Vosges, the Central Plateau of France, Brittany, the south of England and of Ireland, and also Newfoundland, Nova Scotia and, in the United States, all the Appalachian region."

The end of this continental era, thinks M. Termier, came during the Tertiary Period, when the mass, bounded on the south by a chain of mountains, was submerged long before the collapse of those volcanic lands of which the Azores are the last vestiges. The South Atlantic ocean was likewise occupied for many thousands of centuries by a great continent now engulfed beneath the sea. These movements of depression probably occurred at several periods. In the Europe of the Tertiary era the movement was developing which gave rise to the Alpine mountain chain. How far did this chain extend into the Atlantic region ? Did some fragments of it rise high enough to lift themselves for some centuries above the waters ? This question M. Termier answers in the affirmative.

He believes that the geology of the whole Atlantic region has singularly changed in the course of the later periods of the earth's history. During the Secondary Period there were numerous depressions, the Tertiary Period saw the annihilation of the continental areas, and subsequently there appeared a new design, the general direction of which was north and south. Near the African continent, he holds, there have certainly been important movements during Quaternary times, when other changes undoubtedly took place in the true oceanic region. "Geologically speaking," he says, "Plato's account of Atlantis is highly probable. . . . It is entirely reasonable to believe that long after the opening of the Strait of Gibraltar certain of these emerged lands still existed, and among them a marvellous island, separated from the African continent by a chain of other smaller islands."

Professor R. F. Scharff of Dublin concludes that Madeira and the Azores were connected with Portugal in Miocene times, when Man had already appeared in Europe, and that from Morocco to the Canary Islands and thence to South America stretched a vast land which extended southward as far as St. Helena. This great continent, he believes, began to subside before the Miocene or Late Tertiary Period.

Professor Edward Hull is of the opinion that " the flora and fauna of the two hemispheres support the geological theory that there was a common centre in the Atlantic where life began and that during and prior to the glacial epoch great land-bridges north and south spanned the Atlantic Ocean." He adds : " I have made this deduction by a careful study of the soundings as recorded in the Admiralty Charts." Dr. Hull also holds the view that at the time this Atlantic continent existed there was also a great Antillean continent or ridge shutting off the Caribbean Sea and the Gulf of Mexico from the Gulf Stream.

These comprise the most modern conclusions on the subject of Atlantean geology. An equal wealth of biological evidence regarding a former land connection between European and American soil also exists. The European carnivorous animals of Tertiary times show a marked affinity with those of America. The burrowing Amphis-bænidæ, or lizard-snakes, are confined, sixty-four species of them, to America, Africa and the Mediterranean region. Kobelt shows conclusively that the land shells on the two opposite sides of the Atlantic imply an ancient connection having subsisted between the Old World and the New, which became ruptured only during the Miocene epoch of the Tertiary Period. Certain ants occur both in the Azores and America. Sixty per cent of the butterflies and moths found in the Canaries are of Mediterranean origin, and twenty per cent of these are to be found in America. Some crustaceans afford the best proof of an ancient connection between Europe and America.

M. Louis Germain has discovered numerous indications of a close resemblance between the mollusca of Europe, the Canaries and America. He believes that their distri-bution implies the extension of the Atlantic continent to the West Indies in Miocene times, and a separation during the Miocene or near its close, between the West Indian and the Atlantic continents. Says Termier, writing of Germain's deductions: " Two facts remain relative to the marine animals and both seem impossible of explana-tion, except by the persistence up to very nearly the present times, of a maritime shore extending from the West Indies to Senegal, and even binding together Florida, the Bermudas, and the bottom of the Gulf of Guinea. . . . During the Miocene Period, this continent extends as far as the West Indies. It is then portioned off, at first in the direction of the West Indies, then in the south, by the establishment of a marine shore which extends as far as Senegal and to the depths of the Gulf of Guinea, then at length in the east, probably during the Pliocene epoch, along the coast of Africa. The last great fragment, finally engulfed, and no longer having left any other vestiges than the four archipelagoes, would be the Atlantis of Plato."[1]

Summing up the evidence for the former existence of a great continent in the Atlantic stretching from Europe to America, we find that so many geologists and biologists of experience support this theory as to leave practically not a doubt of its authenticity.

The final vestiges of the Atlantean continent would seem to have disappeared, according to the most trustworthy geological opinion at some time not far distant from 10,000 B.C. But what proof have we that Antillia maintained a terrestrial connection with it either by land-bridge or an insular chain at that late date, or at any date when man inhabited the Antillean land-mass ?

We have already seen that geological opinion supports the belief in an Atlantean-Antillean connection in Tertiary times, and that "a maritime shore" or land-bridge persisted "up to very nearly the present time" between the land-masses. This in itself is sufficient to prove our case. The soundings taken in the Atlantic by various Admiralty authorities have revealed the existence of a great bank or elevation commencing near the coast of Ireland, traversed by the fifty-third parallel, and extending in a southerly direction embracing the Azores, to the neighbourhood of French Guiana and the mouths of the Amazon and Para Rivers. The level of this great ridge is some 9000 feet above the bed of the Atlantic. This is, of course, part of the remains of the sunken continent of Atlantis. We have also seen that Scharff believes the Antillean continent to have extended eastward at least as far as the island of Anguilla. This would mean that at the period of their earliest separation Atlantis and Antillia could not have been sundered by any appreciable distance.

It would also seem reasonable to infer from the parallel arrangement and easterly trend of the West India Islands that other islands now submerged formed "stepping-stones" from Antillia to disintegrating Atlantis. The "remote Bermudas" are obviously the remains of continental land. The Antilles notoriously constitute a region of seismic instability, and numerous insular prolongations of the mass of Central America must have risen and become

---

[1] " Annual Report of the Smithsonian Institute for 1915."

C

submerged at intervals throughout all geological time as the result of seismic disturbance.

We can imagine the slow crumbling of Atlantis, its gradual disappearance, the equally gradual migration to Europe on the east and to Antillia on the west, at first by land-bridge, and in a later era by boat and, centuries later, the eventual exodus from Antillian soil to the American mainland after some more than usually disastrous upheaval.

This brings us to the consideration of the question as to whether Atlantis and Antillia had a cultural connection. We can at present speak of Atlantean culture only from what we know of its European manifestations. It is only by employing this evidence in a comparative manner that we can hope to demonstrate that a similar culture existed in Antillia and America. We are already aware that certain plants, animals and mollusca are common to Europe and America, and imply an ancient connection between these continents. We find also that the vestigial traces of Atlantis, the Canary Islands, were peopled at the time of their discovery by the relics of the Crô-Magnon race, a people who invaded Northern Spain and Southern France about 28,000 B.C., the place of whose origin is unknown to modern archæologists, and who, along with subsequent immigrant races to this sphere I believe to have had an Atlantean provenance.

The Crô-Magnons arrived in Europe towards the end of the great Ice Age, and have left fairly plentiful records of their presence in the Biscayan, Pyrenean and Dordogne regions of Spain and France. Their height averaged 6 feet $1\frac{1}{2}$ inches, and the capacity of the brain-case is much superior to that of any known race of man at the present time. The walls of the caverns which they occupied are in many cases covered with drawings of animals and men which, for accuracy of design and modelling have never been surpassed, and which have nothing of the stiffness of Egyptian or Babylonian art in their freedom and spirit. On the walls of these caverns, too, are imprints of human hands which had been placed against the rock and then dusted round with red earth. Similar hand-markings are found in American caves, and were known in ancient Mexico.

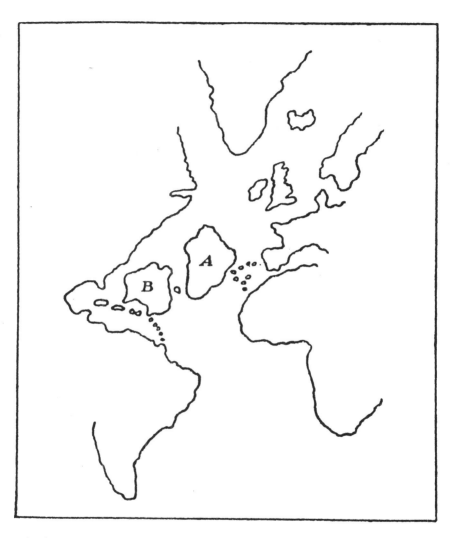

Outline map showing probable relative positions of Atlantis (*A*) and Antillia (*B*) with adjacent islands.

" These people," says Professor Osborn, " were the Palæolithic Greeks. Artistic observation and representation and a true sense of proportion and of beauty were instinctive with them from the beginning."[1] Not only did they draw the mammoth, the bison and the deer on the walls of their caverns, but in bas-reliefs and statuettes they showed a high appreciation of anatomical form. Professor Osborn further remarks that their smaller figures in the round " resemble the work of modern Cubists." This art, which had several phases, is known as Aurignacian,[2] from the French district of Aurignac, where it was first discovered. It flourished from about 23,000 B.C. to 8000 B.C.

Now it is obvious that an art so excellent and highly developed as to have drawn encomiums from all who have examined it cannot have developed in the region where its manifestations are found, for the simple reason that none of its evolutionary phases are encountered there. It is observed in France and Spain in a fully developed state, and it is clear that it must have grown up and persisted elsewhere for thousands of years prior to its first appearance in Europe. Its authors were undoubtedly the parents of European civilisation. Whence did they come ?

The Abbé Breuil, the premier authority on Aurignacian culture, is of opinion that its successive invasions took place either from the south or Mediterranean direction or from the Atlantic coasts of Spain and France. He refuses to contemplate an eastern origin for it.[3] Most authorities are agreed that its earliest signs are to be found in the Dordogne and the Pyrenees, though others uphold an African genesis for it. It is to be observed, however, that Crô-Magnon man first appeared in South-western Europe at a period when widespread subsidences were undoubtedly taking place in the Atlantic area, and that the roots of his culture are not to be discovered on European soil. Its African origin is practically placed out of court by the fact that the earliest Aurignacian stations in Spain and France

---

[1] *Men of the Old Stone Age*, 1915, pp. 315, 316.

[2] The name Aurignacian has become practically interchangeable with that of Crô-Magnon, just as " French " and " Gallic " are interchangeable.

[3] *Les subdivisions du palæolithie supérieur, Cong. Intern. d'Anthrop. Prehist.*, XIVth session, Geneva, 1912, p. 175.

are without exception situated in the Biscayan region, and not on the southern coasts of the peninsula, where one would naturally look for them had they had an African origin.

Professor Osborn reviews the possible relationships between the Crô-Magnon race and the isolated Guanches of the Canary Islands. " Our interest in the fate of the Crô-Magnons is so great that the Guanche theory may also be considered. It is known to be favoured by many anthropologists : von Behr, von Luschan, Mehlis, and especially by Verneau. The Guanches were a race of people who formerly spread all over the Canary Islands, and who preserved their primitive characteristics even after their conquest by Spain in the fifteenth century. The differences from the supposed modern Crô-Magnon man may be mentioned first. The skin of the Guanches is described by the poet Viana as light coloured, and Verneau considers that the hair was blond or light chestnut and the eyes blue. The colouring, however, is somewhat conjectural. The features of resemblance to the ancient Crô-Magnons are numerous. The minimum stature of the men was 5 feet 7 inches, and the maximum 6 feet 7 inches. In one locality the average male stature was over 6 feet. The women were comparatively small. (The Crô-Magnon woman was petite.—Author.) The most striking characters of the head were the fine forehead, the extremely long skull and the pentagonal form of the cranium, when seen from above, caused by the prominence of the parietals—a Crô-Magnon characteristic. . . . The offensive weapons in warfare consisted of three stones, a club and several knives of obsidian. The defensive weapon was a simple lance. The Guanches used wooden swords with great skill. The habitation of all the people was in large well-sheltered caverns, which honeycombed the sides of the mountains. All the walls of these caverns were decorated, the ceilings were covered with a uniform coat of red ochre, while the walls were decorated with various geometric designs in red, black, grey and white. Hollowed-out stones served as lamps. We may conclude with Verneau that there is evidence, although not of a very convincing kind, that the Guanches were related to the Crô-Magnons."[1]

[1] Op. cit., pp. 454, 455.

Dr. Réné Verneau, a skilled French anthropologist, well acquainted with the archæology of the Canaries, states that the Guanches were above all troglodytes. Their caves, he says, were painted like those of the Crô-Magnons. The late Lord Abercromby wrote : " In the museums of the Grand Canary, Teneriffe and Palma a considerable number of prehistoric vessels are preserved. Anthropologists are agreed that the natives of the archipelago at the time of its conquest in the fifteenth century were a composite people, made up of at least three stocks : a Crô-Magnon type, a Hamitic or Berber type and a brachycephalic type. These natives were in a Neolithic state of civilisation."[1]

It is impossible for Crô-Magnon man to have made his way from Europe to the Canaries, both because he possessed no means of navigation and for the simple reason that he was by common consent an immigrant to Europe. Like many of the animals and plants of these vestigial islands, he was cut off and marooned on them by some great natural cataclysm. He must have found his way to Europe by a still existing land-bridge some 25,000 years ago. Says Professor J. L. Myres in *The Cambridge Ancient History* (p. 48) : " The similarity between Aurignacian (i.e. Crô-Magnon) skulls in Europe and the prehistoric skulls in Lagoa Santa in Brazil and other remote localities round the margins of South America, suggests that this type had once almost as wide a distribution as that of the older types of implements." Elsewhere in the same volume we encounter the statement that Crô-Magnon culture was " a well-marked regional culture of the Atlantic coast plain."

About 14,000 B.C., as nearly as can be estimated, Crô-Magnon art took a new phase, which is known as the Magdalenian. This phase exhibits the genius of the Crô-Magnon race at its height, and preceded its sudden decline and disappearance as the dominant type in Europe. " It seems," says Osborn, " like a technical invasion in the history of Western Europe." Breuil observes that " it appears as if the fundamental elements of the superior Aurignacian culture had been contributed by some unknown route to constitute the kernel of the Magdalenian

[1] " Prehistoric Pottery of the Canary Islands," *Nature*, 3rd Dec., 1914.

civilisation." " The Magdalenians," says Osborn, " were newcomers in Western France, but were undoubtedly of Crô-Magnon race." This can only imply that the older Aurignacian art received a stimulus from its original and parent source. " Breuil himself," says Osborn, " has positively stated that the whole Upper Palæolithic art-development of Europe was the work of one race. If so, this race can be none other than the Crô-Magnon."

From this it seems to be clear that the Magdalenian invasion was a further emigration from disintegrating Atlantis. The Magdalenians were of the same ethnological stock as the Crô-Magnons, and introduced an even higher culture than theirs—the " official " culture of Atlantis, from which they had newly come. The Crô-Magnons of France and Spain were thus reinforced by a second wave of immigrants from the old Atlantic home, who had perfected the ancient art common to both in a different sphere. Osborn remarks that this Magdalenian art is at its best equal to that of Egypt and Babylon. An extensive system of trade was in vogue among them. Their civilisation was greatly in advance of that of any presently existing barbarous people.

At a still later epoch, roughly about 8000 B.C., a third race, the Azilian-Tardenoisian, entered Spain and France by *precisely the same route as its predecessors had done*. They had a curious and almost elfin touch in their working of flint implements, and possessed a geometric art which was the prototype of the arabesque. They introduced the bow and arrow into Europe, and painted strange symbols on pebbles. These people were the parents of the great Iberian race and brought with them the culture known as Neolithic or New Stone Age. They invaded Europe at an epoch which synchronises with that given by Plato for the fall of Atlantis. Official archæologists are vague in their statements regarding the place of origin of this race. M. D'Arbois de Jubainville, the well-known Celtic authority, says : " The Iberians seem to be the descendants of those ten millions of legendary warriors who, according to Theopompus, came from a continent separated from ours by the ocean, and established themselves in the country of the Hyperboreans. These were their ancestors, who, leaving Atlantis nine thousand years before Plato, had impressed their domination on Western Europe, Italy and North Africa to the frontiers of Egypt."[1]

If we summarise the foregoing statements we find that the Crô-Magnon, a highly developed race mentally and physically, entered South-western Europe about 25,000 years ago at the close of the Great Ice Age, and during a period of subsidence in the Atlantic. They brought with them an art which must have required centuries of development, and must have been accompanied by a social polity of a high standard. This implies the evolution of their culture elsewhere. There are, indeed, no traces of its infancy in the known world. All the early Aurignacian or Crô-Magnon stations were situated around the Biscayan-Pyrenean region. Their physical constitution and art have been linked by the highest authorities with those of the Guanches of the Canary Islands, the remnant of a sunken continent in the Atlantic, and this suggests that they came from that region at a period of disintegration by way of a land-bridge. Remains strongly resembling those of Crô-Magnon man have been discovered at Lagoa Santa in Brazil and elsewhere in South America. His facial structure closely resembles that of the Red Indians of North America, who, as will be seen later, retains many of his religious and social customs. A second wave of Aurignacian civilisation, the Magdalenian, reached Europe about 14,000 B.C. About 10,000 B.C. a third wave of immigrants appeared in the Biscay region, the Azilian-Tardenoisians, forerunners of the Iberian race. These settled also in North Africa.

Now do we find a similar invasion of American soil by a highly cultured race at such a period as we might well connect with the later submergence of the Antillian portion of the Atlantean continent in which many of the Atlanteans would undoubtedly have taken refuge? It may well have happened that Antillia, as a sub-continent, was not *finally* submerged until some 2100 years ago. The last vestiges of the last land-bridge which connected Britain with Europe existed until 8000 years ago, or, more properly speaking, its main mass then underwent submergence, the Frisian Islands constituting its last remains. As has been said, the Antillean region is one of notorious seismic instability. Be that as it may, we find about the year 200 B.C.

[1] *Les premiers habitants de l'Europe*, pp. 24, 25.

or 2100 years ago, abundant traces of the invasion of American soil by a race possessing the highest artistic capacities of a culture which can in many ways be linked with the Aurignacian. In a word, the phenomenon of the Aurignacian invasion of Europe was repeated on American soil at a later date, and accompanied by the manifestations of an Aurignacian art which had developed during the intervening centuries, as might be expected, but which had never lost its basic resemblance to original forms. Such sudden appearances in Europe and America of cultures so closely allied, though divided by many centuries of time, cannot be fortuitous.

The carriers of the culture in question were the Maya, the origin of whom is, according to archæologists, shrouded in a mystery quite as dense as that which surrounds the provenance of the Aurignacians. That they were Aurignacians, that is Atlanteans, in culture and origin I shall try to demonstrate later. At present it is necessary to furnish some account of their peculiar type of civilisation.

The clearest proof of the Atlantean-Antillian origin of American civilisation is to be found in the culture and traditions of the Maya race of Guatemala, Chiapas and Yucatan. This great and truly advanced people appear suddenly in Central America with a culture fully developed, an elaborate hieroglyphic system, a religion eloquent of high theological concepts, and an architecture which rivals, if it does not surpass, that of Egypt or Sumeria.

The roots of Maya civilisation are not to be encountered on American soil. No steps in the evolution of their writing, religion or architecture can be traced in the regions in which their monuments are found, and though competent authorities recognise new phases and aspects in their art-forms subsequent to their entrance to Central America, the complete absence of all primary evolutionary forms proves conclusively that Maya art was not originally conceived on American soil. Where not a link with the humbler forms of art, handicraft or custom is to be found, it seems only rational to look for the beginnings of their culture and art elsewhere.

Indeed, the very earliest specimens of Maya art, architecture and handicraft known to us exhibit the sure traces of degeneration. Here is an art and a philosophy so rich, so overripe, as to approach senility and disintegration. Its forms were stereotyped, its ideas rooted in convention. Its society resembled that of the China of half a century ago, a community passionately conservative in its ideals, hastening to decay.

Maya civilisation makes its first appearance in Central America in the centuries immediately preceding the Christian era, roughly about 200 B.C. Its earliest dated monuments cannot with safety be ascribed to a more remote period. No sooner did it take root in Central American soil than it began to send forth vigorous shoots. Regarding the precise place of its first settlement, authoritative opinion is practically agreed. The general character of the architectural remains in the region lying between the Bay of Tabasco and the foot of the Cordilleras, and watered by the River Usumacinta and the Rio de la Pasion in the modern state of Chiapas, points almost conclusively to this district as the cradle of Central American culture, and the relatively archaic type of the hieroglyphs found upon its monuments as well as the early dates these contain, give to this theory something of finality. The oldest known centres of Maya life are probably Tikal and Peten in Eastern Guatemala. It is believed that the development of the Maya states in Chiapas and Guatemala continued for seven or eight hundred years, or until the close of the sixth century A.D., about which time disaster seems to have come upon them with tragic suddenness.

We do not know the cause of the downfall of what must have been a complex and highly developed civilisation. Possibly a horde of barbarians from the North swept down upon these settled communities. But even to-day its gorgeous temples and palaces show no signs of deliberate destruction such as surely would have been evident had they fallen into the hands of savages. More probably these cities were emptied of their inhabitants by one of the migratory impulses which so frequently reappear in American aboriginal history. In all likelihood their gods ordained an exodus. The theory of a wholesale migration is rendered probable by the fact that the period of desertion synchronises with that of the discovery of the Maya of the peninsula of Yucatan, a region whose wealth in stone must have attracted a nation of stone builders. But Yucatan is on the whole an arid country, and it is likely that the retreat of the Maya thence was dictated by the imperative reason of self-preservation.

The most important of the older city-states were Palenque, Piedras Negras, Ocosingo, Tikal, Yaxchilan and Quirigua, sites which are scattered over Southern Mexico and Guatemala, while Copan, perhaps the greatest of all, is situated in Honduras, the southern limit of Maya culture, so far as is presently known. Of the later sites in Yucatan, Chichen Itzá was by far the most famous, Mayapan, Uxmal and Labna barely approaching it in celebrity.

With the discovery of Yucatan a new era opened up for Maya art and social activity. At first the bare struggle for existence on the inhospitable and poorly irrigated plateau was probably intense. But the ingenious immigrants triumphed over conditions of the most formidable kind, and by degrees improved their architectural knowledge and astronomical science, fixing the revolutionary period of the planets with accuracy, and developing the solar calendar. A Maya Renaissance was fully under way by the end of the tenth century, and edifices which recall the palmy days of Palenque and Copan were once more rising over all Yucatan. About the year A.D. 1000 Chichen Itzá, Uxmal and Copan formed a political confederacy, and under the pacific conditions which followed the institution of this league, art and science blossomed forth anew. Cities multiplied with astonishing rapidity, and the art of sculpture, which had now become merely an adjunct to architecture, achieved an elaboration and intricacy of design unsurpassed, perhaps, by any people in any age.

With the disruption of what may be called the Triple Alliance, about the year 1200, an event precipitated by the conspiracy of the ruler of Chichen Itzá against his colleague of Mayapan, a series of disastrous wars ensued which lasted until the country was discovered by the Spaniards. These endless internecine struggles led to the employment of mercenaries from the ruder tribes of Mexico, whose presence set an indelible stamp upon Maya art and manners, and we find the Maya sculptors forced to carry out the designs of a Mexican military aristocracy, even accompanying them with the completely different hieroglyphical inscriptions of the usurpers. Had they placed side by side with them the equivalent Maya characters, modern science would have been equipped with an American Rosetta Stone, as the Mexican glyphs, unlike those of the Maya, can now be deciphered with a reasonable degree of exactitude.

This brings us to the problem of Maya writing, the precise character of which has not as yet been definitely arrived at. For the pursuit of this quest a far greater degree of industry and ingenuity has been needful than for the decipherment of the ancient writings of Egypt or Sumeria. Certain of the " calculiform " or pebble-shaped characters found on stelæ and the walls of temples have been unriddled, especially those which apply to the sun, moon and planets, those for " beginning " and " ending," the symbols for the year, " night," and some others. The most important texts, strangely enough, are connected with the regions of the older settlements in Guatemala and Chiapas rather than with Yucatan, and in the three Maya manuscripts which remain to us—the Dresden, Paris and Madrid MSS.—the glyphs appear as a number of small squares rounded at the corners and representing human faces and other objects highly conventionalised by generations of artistic usage and development. They are arranged, as a rule, in two parallel columns and are read two columns at a time, from left to right and from top to bottom. For a long time it was believed that the work of Landa, Bishop of Yucatan, contained the key to the script. But it is now known that the natives, exasperated by his destruction of their manuscripts, deliberately deceived him, and that with the exception of the symbols for the days and " months " his key is quite misleading.

Much difference of opinion exists as to whether the system is phonetic or ideographic in character. It is probably both phonetic and pictorial to some extent, but for the most part it appears to be of the nature of rebus writing, in which the characters do not indicate the meaning of the objects which they portray, but only the sounds of their names. Thus, if English were written in this manner, the picture of a human eye might stand for the first personal pronoun, a drawing of a bee for the verb " to be," and so forth. But it seems probable that an increasing number of phonetic elements will be identified, though the idea of a glyph will always be found to over-

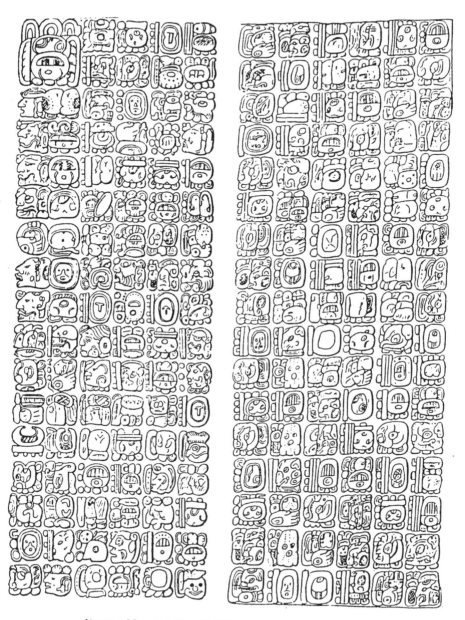

PLATE II.—MAYA HIEROGLYPHIC SCRIPT.
Inscription on the tablet of the cross, Palenque.

shadow its phonetic value. Through generations of use the system came to possess a significance entirely ideographic, and would not necessitate any such effort of mental translation as a people unused to rebus writing would have to make to comprehend it readily.

The manner in which the arithmetical and chronological system of the Maya was discovered is decidedly the greatest triumph of American archæology within recent years. A dot stood for one, and a bar or line for five. By various combinations of these the Maya expressed all the numerals from 1 to 19 inclusive. Twenty was denoted by the moon, as indicating the number of days in which the moon waxes and wanes. But the manner in which the " higher mathematics " of the Maya was evolved is much too intricate a process to be described in this place. Some of the periods of time in use among the Maya were based upon the period of revolution of the planet Venus, and were represented by an appropriate hieroglyph, and when a date was sculptured on a monument, the number of periods contained, years, months or moons, and days, were set forth in the glyph which denoted them. These dates can be collated with European chronology through the agency of manuscripts known as " The Books of Chilan Balam," or " The Tiger Priesthood," native annals of the priestly hierarchy of Yucatan, in which the ancient system of chronology is preserved. These annals were fortunately continued into the post-Conquest Period, so that some of the events they date in the native manner have known European equivalents. By the aid of these we can reduce the Maya system of computing time to the terms of our own, and it becomes possible to interpret the dates on the monuments with only a small margin of probable error. Thus the period of the foundation of the city of Palenque has been fixed at 15 B.C., that of Yaxchilan at 75 B.C., Copan A.D. 34, Piedras Negras A.D. 109, and the abandonment of Copan and Quirigua at A.D. 231 and A.D. 292 respectively.

The Antillean origin of the Maya civilisation has been stressed by many authorities, who believed their culture to have had its beginnings in the West Indies. Columbus alludes to the peaceable and civilised character of the inhabitants of these islands. They possessed very con-

siderable maritime skill, and those of the Bahamas had a
regular commerce with Florida.   The Caribs of the Lesser
Antilles penetrated to the heart of Brazil and strongly
resembled the Maya in appearance and culture.   Both
flattened the skull in infancy, had the same burial customs,
and some of the gods of the Antilles strongly resemble
those of the Maya.   The Maya language, too, has been
classified by Beuchat and others as of Antillean origin.

But perhaps the best and most sufficient test of the
relationship of the Maya and Mexicans with the Antillean
region is to be discovered in the surprising traditions they
have left us which refer to their colonisation of Central
America and Mexico.

A wealth of tradition regarding a westerly and trans-
oceanic connection existed in ancient Mexico and Central
America.   This centred round the great mythic figure of
the culture-hero Quetzalcoatl (Feathered-snake) and his
people the Toltecs, the civilising race who are believed to
have entered Mexico in peaceful invasion, and to have
sown the seeds of culture among its barbarous peoples.

The Toltec race appear to have formed the nucleus of a
civilised state in Mexico, and while we encounter Quetzalcoatl as a divinity among the Maya under the names
Gucumatz and Kukulkan, which are merely trans-
lations of his Mexican appellation, we find the Toltecs
occasionally identified by native chroniclers with the
populations of Guatemala or Yucatan.   We find that
Mexican mercenaries attained in the eleventh century A.D.
to much the same degree of power in the Yucatec state of
Chichen Itzá as the alien Janissaries in Constantinople or
the stranger Mamelukes in seventeenth-century Egypt.
Toltec art, too, is found invading the Maya sphere about
the same period.   But that Toltec and Maya were originally
one and the same admits of little dubiety.   The differences
between their beliefs, arts and social customs were merely
such as might have arisen out of a few centuries of
separation.

We see then :

(1) That many geologists of standing credit the existence
of a former Atlantean continent.   Others do not, but, in
the main, offer no good reasons against the hypothesis.

(2) That Atlantis and Antillia must have been at one

period joined in one land-mass, and at a later period by land-bridge or by an insular chain, which permitted the spread of culture from one to the other.

(3) That just as the Atlanteans settled in Europe, they likewise settled in America. The sudden appearance of the Maya people in Central America from the East with a ready-made culture shows conclusively that they were not of mainland stock. Indeed, authorities are at one in attributing an Antillean origin to them.

CHAPTER III

QUETZALCOATL THE ATLANTEAN

WHO, then, were the Toltecs ? Whence did they come ? What answers have archæology and tradition to give to these questions ?

Brinton and the older writers believed them to be wholly fabulous. But recent research has put this theory quite out of court, and a reaction in favour of Toltec authenticity has set in. The monumental and other remains of a race boasting a high standard of culture have been discovered in certain parts of Mexico. Tradition and early written history persistently ascribe these to the Toltecs. The word " Toltec " means " the cultured " or the " civilised people," the builders, the makers of things. Their very name, then, associates them with the pre-Aztec ruins and antiquities of Mexico.

Formerly, I admit, I fully believed that the Toltecs were mythical. But as time progressed and the spade unearthed proof after proof of the presence of a civilised pre-Aztec race in Mexico at sites which early local tradition associated with the Toltec name, I was forced into acceptance of the conclusions of Manuel Gamio and others that a definite historical basis underlay the Toltec " fable." To Professor Eduard Seler, the foremost among Americanists, the Toltecs were a Mexican race who arrived in Mexico during the seventh century of our era, pushing their way up the coast from Yucatan or Guatemala, where they had already exercised a civilising influence. For Lehmann, another careful authority, Toltec chronicle was a melange of myth and history, but he did not believe that " the question of the difficult problem of the origin of the Toltecs " was actually solved.

But the later researches of Manuel Gamio and others have made it clear enough that we must allow the Toltecs a local habitation and a name. It has been shown that the sites of Tollan, Cholula and Teotihuacan are undoubtedly of Toltec origin. Mr. T. Athol Joyce in his *Mexican Archæology* cannot see why the name Toltec should be refused to this culture, and indeed there is no good reason to refuse it. E. J. Payne in his monumental *History of the New World* gives it as his opinion that " the accounts of Toltec history current at the Conquest contain a nucleus of substantial truth," and concludes that " to doubt that there once existed in Tollan an advancement superior to that which prevailed among the Nahuatlaca (that is the pre-Aztec tribes) generally at the Conquest, and that its people spread their advancement throughout Anahuac (Mexico) and into the districts eastward and southward, would be to reject a belief universally entertained, and confirmed rather than shaken by the efforts made in later times to construct for the Pueblo something in the nature of a history."

If, then, we grant an actual existence to the Toltecs on archæological grounds, we shall find these greatly strengthened by the traditions associated with these people. Ixtlilxochitl, a native chronicler who lived shortly after the Conquest of Mexico by Cortes, and who had exceptional opportunities for obtaining good information, states in his *Historia Chichimeca* that the Toltecs did not set out to colonise distant countries from any impulse of their own, but were the victims of internecine dissension in the homeland, and had perforce to seek their fortunes elsewhere. Thus thrust forth, they set their faces southward, and reached a place called Tlapallan in the year A.D. 387. Passing the country of Xalisco, they effected a landing at Huatulco, and journeyed down the coast of Mexico until they reached Tochtepec, whence they pushed inland toward Tollan. It took them no less than 104 years to make this journey. In another work, the *Relaciones*, he gives a totally different account of the Toltec migrations. He tells us that the chiefs of Tlapallan had revolted against the royal authority and were banished from that region in A.D. 439.[1] Lingering near their ancient territory for the space of eight years, they then journeyed to Tlapallant-zinco, where they halted for three hundred years before setting out on a prolonged pilgrimage which occupied the tribe for more than a century.

In his *Monarquia Indiana* Torquemada says of the Toltecs that they were a body of men who came from the north by way of Panuco, dressed in robes of black linen, cut low at the neck, and with short sleeves. They came to Tollan, but finding the country there too thickly peopled,

[1] These dates cannot be accepted as trustworthy. Veytia believes Tollan to have been founded in A.D. 713.

passed on to Cholula, where they were well received. Their chief was Quetzalcoatl, a man with ruddy complexion and long beard. They multiplied, and sent colonies to the Mixtec and Zapotec countries, in the south-west, raising the great buildings at Mitla. They were cunning handicraftsmen, not so good at masonry as at jeweller's work, sculpture and agriculture.

Here it should be remarked that the history of Tollan, the city founded on Mexican soil by the Toltecs, bears a close resemblance to that of Atlantis. Ixtlilxochitl says that it was founded by the Toltecs in the year A.D. 566. This city, the site of which is now occupied by the modern town of Tula, was situated north-west of the mountains which bound the Mexican valley. It required six years to erect the magnificent palaces and temples of which it was composed. The valley in which it stood was known as " The Place of Fruits " because of its surprising fertility. The Toltecs made rapid progress in the various arts, and their settlement came to be celebrated far and wide for the excellence of its craftsmen and the beauty of its architecture and pottery. The very walls were encrusted with rare red and black stones, and their masonry was so beautifully chiselled and laid as to resemble the choicest mosaic.

A line of able kings succeeded the founder of the Toltec monarchy, until in A.D. 994, according to Ixtlilxochitl, the degenerate Huemac II ascended the throne of Tollan. At first he ruled with wisdom, but later he fell from the high place he had made for himself in the regard of the people by reason of his faithless deception of them and his licentious habits. The provinces rose in revolt, and many signs and gloomy omens foretold the downfall of the city. As in the case of Atlantis, its inhabitants had incurred the wrath of the gods by their love of pleasure and selfishness, and a similar fate befell them. In the winter which ensued such a severe frost visited the land that all crops and plants were killed. A summer of torrid heat followed, so intense in its suffocating fierceness that the streams were dried up and the very rocks melted. Plagues completed the ruin. In the event the degenerate Toltecs were driven out of the land by the warlike Chichimec tribes of the northern steppes. Mexico knew them no more, and their name and

PLATE III: HOUSE OF THE GOVERNOR, UXMAL, YUCATAN

Specimen of Maya architecture.

culture lingered only as a legend in the vicinity of the
proud cities they had raised.[1]

Now it is obvious that these occurrences did not happen
on Mexican soil. Frost seldom visits these latitudes, and
never with such severity as this legend relates. It is at
least equally true that rocks do not melt, even in the
torrid sun of Mexico. But they do under the influence of
earthquake or other seismic disturbance or volcanic agency,
of which I believe this tale to be a reminiscence, adapted
to the circumstances of the Toltec political break-up under
the pressure of the more virile northern tribes. In fact it
is pretty clear from this account that a much more venerable myth of catastrophe in another land has been confounded with the history of the Toltec downfall. The
experiences of the defeated and scattered Toltecs, who
appear to have betaken themselves to Yucatan and
Guatemala on the destruction of their city, became
entangled with another and older story which they re-
counted of their evacuation of another region. That to
me seems very clear. The tale of the downfall of Tollan
has become interwoven with that of the cataclysm of
Tlapallan, or as some writers actually call it, Tollan-
Tlapallan, the place whence they originally came, and
Tollan the First and Tollan the Second were, in the circumstances of their destruction at least, confused in the
Toltec mind, or, perhaps in the minds of later Mexican
chroniclers.

As I have said, one personage is associated with the
Toltecs who undoubtedly links them with Atlantis-Antillia.
This is the culture-hero Quetzalcoatl, who first led them
into the country, and who finally returned to the homeland
whence he had come. A bewildering array of myths
cluster around his personality, and in dealing with them
we must exercise selection very carefully if we are to
combine them into such a reasoned narrative as will prove
useful in our investigation. I shall, in the first place,
summarise these important myths, and at a later stage try
to glean from them their real significance. The myth of
Quetzalcoatl has been handled (mishandled would be the

---

[1] No good modern résumé of the Toltec question exists; but see
Brinton, " Were the Toltecs an Historic Nationality ? " (*Proc. Am. Phil.
Soc.*, XXIV, pp. 229–41, 1887).

better term) by generations of writers on the subject of Atlantis. But perhaps the thirty years of study I have devoted to it will assist me to excogitate its true relationship to the Atlantean hypothesis.[1]

We will see that Quetzalcoatl was regarded as the leader of the immigrant Maya into Central America about 200 B.C. and as the chief of the Toltecs who invaded Mexico some eight hundred years later. But this merely implies that the myth was carried into Mexico by Maya-Toltecs who naturalised it there, just as the myth of Arthur was carried from one centre into all the Celtic countries.

The " standard " account of Quetzalcoatl is that given by Sahagun, a careful and painstaking clerical writer who flourished in Mexico about the middle of the sixteenth century, who deals with the nature of this god or culture-hero in the Third Book of his *Historia Universal de Nueva España*. Quetzalcoatl, says Sahagun, was the father of the arts. His houses were made of native jadeite, silver, white and red shells and feathers. His servants were known as " the Swift Ones who serrate the teeth." The land was wealthy in his time, and a head of maize was a burden for a strong man. He did penance by drawing blood with the spines of the maguey plant, and by bathing at midnight. But the native sorcerers, Tezcatlipoca and Uitzilopochtli, were jealous of him and minded to destroy him. Tezcatlipoca came to his palace disguised as a physician, and, hearing that he was sick, proffered him a magical draught which, he assured Quetzalcoatl, would make him forget his sorrows and his strong desire to leave Mexico. Quetzalcoatl, seeing that his secret had been probed, asked the mysterious visitant where he must betake himself. " To Tollan-Tlapallan," was the reply, " where another old man awaits thee. He and you shall speak together, and on thy return thou shalt be as a youth, yes, even as a boy."

Quetzalcoatl drank the medicine, though doubtfully, and in time became intoxicated. So great a longing to depart came upon him that at length he arose and went from Tollan. Arrived at the coast, he commanded that a raft of serpents should be constructed for him, and in this

[1] A fuller dissertation of the Quetzalcoatl myth will be found in my *Gods of Mexico*, pp. 117–45.

he seated himself as in a canoe, put out to sea, and set out on his voyage to Tollan-Tlapallan.

Torquemada, another monkish writer, in his account of the myth of Quetzalcoatl borrows largely from Sahagun, but states that Sahagun, when at Xochimilco, was asked by the natives, who were keenly desirous of knowledge on the point, where Tlapallan was. He replied that he did not know, as he had not then been long among them. Torquemada proceeds to say that when Quetzalcoatl departed, he assured his disciples that at a future time there would come by the way of the sea, where the sun

Quetzalcoatl, from the Mexican Codex Borgia.

rises, certain white men with black beards, like him, and that these would be his brothers and would rule the land.

The interpreter of the Codex Telleriano-Remensis, a document painted by Aztec scribes at the request of certain Spanish priests, says of Quetzalcoatl, " Quetzalcoatl, they say, was he who created the world. And they bestowed upon him the appellation of Lord of the Wind, because they say that Tonacatecutli, when it appeared good to him, breathed and begat Quetzalcoatl. . . . They cele-brated a festival on the sign of the four earthquakes to the destroyer, with reference to the fate which again waited the world : for they said that it had undergone four destructions and would again be destroyed. He alone

had a human body like that of men. The other gods were
of an incorporeal nature. After the deluge the custom
of sacrificing commenced. . . . They name him 'One
Cane,' which is the star Venus, of which they tell the
fable accredited among them. Tlauizcalpan Tecutli is the
star Venus, the first created light before the deluge. This
star is Quetzalcoatl."[1]

The interpreter of the Codex Vaticanus A., a similar
document, says : " He it was, as they say, who caused
hurricanes, and in my opinion was the god who was called
Citaladuali, and it was he who destroyed the world by
winds. . . . The son of the virgin, Quetzalcoatl, knowing
that the vices of men were necessarily the cause of the
troubles of the world, determined on asking the goddess
Chalchihuitlicue who is she who remained after the deluge
with the man in the tree (ark), and is the mother of the
god Tlaloc, whom they have made goddess of water, that
they might obtain rain when they stood in need of it. . . .
Of Quetzalcoatl they relate that, proceeding on his journey,
he arrived at the Red Sea, which is here painted, and which
they named Tlapallan, and that on entering into it they
saw no more of him nor knew what became of him. . . .
They say that it was he who effected the reformation of
the world by penance, since as, according to his account,
his father had created the world and men had given
themselves up to vice, on which account it had frequently
been destroyed, Citinatonali sent his son into the world
to reform it. . . . They celebrated a great festival on this
sign, as we shall see on the sign of four earthquakes, because
they feared that the world would be destroyed in that
sign (or date) as he had foretold them when he disappeared
in the Red Sea, which event occurred on the same sign."[2]

As I will try to show later, we have here a number of
allusions to a condition closely resembling the groundwork
of the Atlantis myth. But resemblances even more start-
ling come to light when we examine those myths regarding
Quetzalcoatl which were current in Guatemala and
Yucatan.

[1] This Codex is reproduced in Kingsborough's *Antiquities of Mexico*,
Vol. VI, pp. 95–153.
[2] Reproduced in Kingsborough's *Antiquities of Mexico*, Vol. VI,
pp. 155–420.

A book in the language of the Quiche Indians of Guatemala, said to have been written by Votan, a local name for Quetzalcoatl, was at one time in the possession of Nuñez de la Vega, Bishop of Chiapas, who introduced portions of it into his *Constituciones Diocesianos de Chiapas*, yet, with the intolerance of his age, destroyed the priceless original in his holocaust of manuscripts and paintings of native origin at Huehuetlan in 1691. A certain Ordoñez de Aguilar had, however, made a copy of it before its destruction, and incorporated it in his *Historia de Cielo* MS. In this work Votan declares himself " a snake," the descendant of Imos, of the line of Chan, a tribe of Lacandone Indians situated near Palenque, who, he says, were of the race of Chivim. Taking Aguilar's account along with that of de la Vega, as both rely on the same authority, we find that Votan (that is Quetzalcoatl) proceeded to America by divine command, his mission being to lay the foundations of civilisation in that land. With this object in view, he left the land of Valum Chivim, passed the dwelling of the Thirteen Snakes, and arrived in Valum Votan, whence, with several members of his family, he set out to form a settlement, ascending the Usumacinta River and ultimately founding Palenque. Because of the strange dress they wore, the Tzendal Indians whom they encountered called the colonists Tzequitles, or " Men with Shirts," but agreed to form a pact with them. Votan, having established himself at Palenque, made several visits to his original home. On one of these he came to a tower which had been intended to reach the heavens, a project which had been confounded by the diversity of language among those who conceived it. He was permitted to reach " the rock of heaven " by a subterranean passage, and returning to Palenque, discovered that others of his race had arrived there with whom he made an amicable agreement. He built a temple by the Huehuetan River, known from its subterranean chambers as " The House of Darkness," and here he deposited the national records in the care of certain old men called *tlapianes*, or guardians, and an order of priestesses. Nuñez de la Vega's work contains the following illuminating passage on this most interesting retreat :

" Votan is the third heathen in the calendar (that is,

the deity who is ascribed to the third division of the Maya calendar), and in the little history written in the Indian language all the provinces and cities in which he tarried are mentioned ; and to this day there is always a clan in the city of Teopisa which they call the Votans. They say that he saw the great wall, namely, the Tower of Babel, which was built from earth to heaven at the bidding of his grandfather Noah ; and that he was the first man whom God sent to divide and apportion this country of India, and that there, where he saw the great wall, he gave to every nation its special language. It is related that he tarried in Huehueta (which is a city in Soconusco) and that there he placed a tapir and a great treasure in a subterranean house, which he built by the breath of his nostrils, and he appointed a woman as chieftain, with tapianes to guard her. This treasure consisted of jars which were closed with covers of the same clay, and of a room in which the picture of the ancient heathens who are in the calendar were engraved in stone, together with chalchiuites (which are small, heavy, green stones) and other superstitious images ; and the chieftainess herself and the tapianes, her guardians, surrendered all these things, which were publicly burned in the market-place at Huehueta when we inspected the aforesaid province in 1691."

I believe that a careful perusal and criticism of the cycle of myths associated with Quetzalcoatl will greatly assist us to a better comprehension of the American relationships of the Atlantean tradition. We observe in them the persistent memory of the arrival of a civilised race from the east, led by a chieftain of striking personality. Doubtless much of pure myth has in the course of centuries attached itself to them with that barnacle-like affinity it possesses for all historic fact—witness the myths which have accreted round the personality of the late Lord Kitchener —but the substratum of reality survives, and is capable of disentanglement from the superincumbent mass of fictional detail. That such a civilised race as these legends speak of actually did arrive on American soil we know. The Maya appear in Central America about 200 B.C. in possession of a fully developed civilisation, a system of writing, a knowledge of masonry, a close acquaintance with the forms of art which it is ridiculous to refer to a social evolution of less than a score of centuries.

We know nothing of the geological history of the West Indian area of 2100 years ago. The occurrence of such terrific cataclysms as that of Mont Pelée, which took place in that region in our own time, illustrates the possibility of similar seismic disturbances on a large scale having occurred at any epoch in the past history of a locality so notoriously unstable. It is highly improbable that a myth like that of Quetzalcoatl, eloquent as it is of the circumstances of forced departure from an eastern oceanic area, should coincide so exactly with the sudden appearance of the Maya in Central America unless some basis of fact underlay it. The Maya themselves spoke of Quetzalcoatl as the founder of their civilisation, calling him Gucumatz, Kukulkan and Votan, and that they drew the greater part of their religious tradition from the faith which he introduced, no student of Maya archæology would deny.

Moreover, as has been said, the resemblance between the tale of the destruction of Tollan, that city connected with Quetzalcoatl and the Toltecs, is more than suspicious. Plato says of Atlantis that gradually the blood of the gods which flowed in the veins of the Atlanteans was diluted with the mortal admixture, and that thereby they grew degenerate. Zeus regarded them with disfavour. Plato's account concludes with the statement that the god was about to gather them together to reproach them with their worldly selfishness and love of pleasure. The sequel in his *Timæus* shows that the divine counsel had not been accepted, and that Zeus had been compelled to destroy them in their wickedness by sending upon them earthquakes, floods and rains, which brought about the complete destruction of their country. In like manner disaster comes upon the Toltecs, but, as I have shown, the circumstances of the myth do not square with what we know of the actual downfall of Tollan, which succumbed to the attacks of the Chichimec Indians of the northern steppes. This implies that that part of the myth which obviously relates to seismic disturbance, should be referred back to a still older legend current in Tollan of disaster in an earlier home, with which it became confused. The very fact that the Toltec called the eastern oceanic country from which

Quetzalcoatl came Tollan-Tlapallan, shows that they had either called their city by the name of the older settlement or that it had in some way become confounded with the maritime country alluded to.

The description of Toltec architecture in these legends bears a striking similarity to what Plato has to say of the Atlantean masonry. The stones of which the Atlanteans constructed their buildings were, he says, white, black and red in colour, and in many of their houses and temples these were intermingled in a striking decorative scheme. They also employed for building a substance known as orichalcum (copper), which emitted red light. If this account be compared with the statements of Ixtlilxochitl and others regarding the colour-schemes of Toltec architecture, the resemblance between the edifices of Atlantis and Tollan is not far to seek.

Let us note, too, that the priestly interpreters of the Mexican Codex Vaticanus A. and the Codex Telleriano-Remensis lay stress upon the relationship of Quetzalcoatl with earthquakes, rains and deluge. The first-mentioned writer states that he caused hurricanes and destroyed the world by winds, and that in his " sign " the Mexicans celebrated the feast of the Four Earthquakes. The interpreter of the Codex Telleriano-Remensis repeats this latter statement, and adds that Quetzalcoatl was connected with the idea of the deluge. Now the power to cause seismic disturbances is regarded by some peoples as residing in the person of the priest-king or chief. Professor J. Macmillan Brown of Christchurch, New Zealand, in his recent fascinating volume *The Riddle of the Pacific*,[1] says that " on the east coast of the island of Yap there is a village called Gatsepar, and its chief, though of no significance or power in his own island, has canoes come over hundreds of miles of sea to pay him annual tribute ; when the tributaries are asked why they do so to so powerless a chief, they say that if they did not keep paying the tribute he would shake their island with his earthquakes and the sea with his tempests. The meaning seems to be that his ancestors built an island-empire to the east of Yap, and when some intermediate islets had gone down the others continued to look still to the ruler in the west as the holder

[1] P. 53.

of all power, natural and supernatural." This illustration
of a custom still obtaining appears to throw a flood of light
not only on the reason for Quetzalcoatl's connection with
earthquakes and tempests but on the Atlantean-Antillian
connection of the Maya civilisation, which evidently, like
its Pacific parallel, looked back to an older culture in a
sunken land.

Quetzalcoatl, then, may have been an Antillian chief
who was regarded as having the power to create seismic
disturbances, and in the passage of time this magical power
to destroy may naturally have come to be confused with
the circumstances of the destruction of Antillia itself.
Quetzalcoatl, it will be noted, is also mentioned by the
interpreter of the Codex Vaticanus A. as having " destroyed
the world by wind."[1]

Although worshipped by the Mexicans and the Maya
of Central America, Quetzalcoatl was still regarded by
them not only as a god but as a man. The whole of his
myth, indeed, is eloquent of his humanity. " He alone,"
says the Codex Telleriano-Remensis, " had a human body
like that of men. The other gods were of an incorporeal
nature." The details of his legend are, indeed, much too
precise for reference to any mere shadowy divinity. He
was, we are told, sent by his father Citinatonali to reform
the world by penance. Such a task might well have been
laid upon an Antillian chief or leader by an offended god,
whose votary might equally readily conceive the notion of
placating him in such a way.

Let us glance for a moment at this god, the father of
Quetzalcoatl, Citinatonali or Citallatonali. He was
regarded by the Mexicans as the creator of heaven and
earth and of mankind. " They painted him alone with
a crown as lord of all." He is in Mexican mythology
" the Very Old One." An ancient Mexican song says that
Quetzalcoatl dedicated a special cult to him. He was unquestionably a god of the Toltecs, accepted at a later period
by the Mexicans. He is represented by the sign cipactli,
the dragon or whale from which the earth was made, and
which rose out of the sea. In Maya myth he is called " the
Old Serpent who is covered with green feathers and who

---

[1] As I show later, the symbol, of Quetzalcoatl was the thunder-stone,
the symbol of seismic disturbance.

lies in the ocean." That is, he is the Maya form of a god
of the sea like Poseidon, the mythical founder of Atlantis,
according to Plato, and father of Atlas.   Citallatonali's
wife was Citlallinicue or Coatlicue, a name which, it may
be observed in passing, looks very like a Mexican attempt
to pronounce the name of Cleito, the name of the maiden
of Atlantis whom Poseidon wooed and married, and who
bore him Atlas and other twin sons.

With almost equal certainty Quetzalcoatl can be
collated with Atlas himself.   In architecture he is represented in caryatid form, for example in a statuette found
in Mexico City in 1900, at Chichen Itzá and elsewhere in

Quetzalcoatl upholding the heavens.

Mexico and Central America, and in many Mexican MSS.
In these, it is especially to be remarked, he is represented,
like Atlas, as bearing the world or the sky on his head.
Dr. H. J. Spinden, an eminent authority on Maya archæology, calls these figures " Atlantean " because of their
resemblance to the Greek caryatids of Atlas.   Quetzalcoatl
is also one of the four Mexican world-supporters, and is
represented in this form in the Aztec Codex Borgia and the
Codex Vaticanus B.   It is clear, too, from his name, " Heart
of the Sea," that he was in some way connected with the
ocean, and this is strengthened by the fact that Chalchihuitlicue, his wife, is goddess of the sea.   Like Atlas, too,
Quetzalcoatl was a twin.

But Quetzalcoatl bequeathed more than a memory to

posterity. We are informed that he was the progenitor of the clan or sect of Votan, the Votanides, to whom Nuñez alludes. He was also the founder of Palenque. The date of the foundation of Palenque has recently been fixed by a competent scholar at 15 B.C., and by another at A.D. 73, from a reading of the calendar dates on the stelæ there. This gives us a more or less definite date to found upon. Palenque may, indeed, be described as the city of Quetzalcoatl, for not only is the feathered serpent, his symbol, ubiquitous there, but the site was assuredly one of the chief centres of his cult in Central America. Tradition, therefore, was surely not at fault in attributing its foundation to him. That part of his legend which alludes to his meeting with the Tzendal Indians, who described his followers as " the Men with Shirts," bears the impress of reality. Once established at Palenque, we are informed that he made several visits to his original home. This would seem to imply that at this period the country of Tollan-Tlapallan had not altogether been submerged, or at least that Quetzalcoatl was compelled to return thither for some more or less powerful reason. His wanderings and voyages are described, and we learn that after his return to Palenque he found other colonists of his own race awaiting him. Finally he deposited his books and other treasures in a subterranean chamber in Huehuetenango in the Quiche country, where they were actually discovered by Bishop Nuñez de la Vega, who, after copying the MSS., destroyed them, along with the images and other insignia which had been treasured there, the last vestiges of Atlantean civilisation.

One of the outstanding discoveries in connection with primitive religion which has been made in recent times is that of Sir James Frazer regarding the magical significance of early kingship. In the personality of the king, it has been found, resided those magical virtues of vitality and virility which were thought to cause the crops to flourish, and the lack of which in a monarch meant agricultural failure. This, of course, dated from a period when the king and the rain-making priest were one and the same individual. Aged and impotent monarchs in an early stage of society, and especially in Egypt and Polynesia, were immolated for the twofold reason that the gods might be placated and a more vigorous successor fulfil their functions. Failing sacrifice, they must be rejuvenated by a magical elixir.

Some such process, I believe, is involved in the myth of Quetzalcoatl. Indeed, in one of the myths which allude to him he is spoken of as being immolated on a funeral pyre. In his time the maize crop was so large and fruitful that only a strong man might carry a head of the cereal of which Quetzalcoatl was the original discoverer. His powers diminish through age, and he conceives the idea of obtaining magical assistance from the fatherland, where, he is assured, " another old man " awaits him, perhaps the high priest of his cult. The expression " another " makes it clear that Quetzalcoatl was at that time regarded as old, but he is assured that he will return " as a youth, yea as a boy " if he will seek aid in the homeland, the one locality where he can obtain the elixir of youth. In the nature-allegory which has been woven out of Quetzalcoatl's history he is thought of as the trade wind which, after bearing the fertilising rains to Mexico, returns to its home in the east to seek new showers to continue its mission in the ensuing spring. But, if I am not in error, the myth contains also a human and historical element, the story of a priest-king forced to return to his ancestral home, partially ruined as that may have been, to seek the aid of its official magics. There are records, as we have seen, of occasional voyages eastward in the myths of Quetzalcoatl to Tollan-Tlapallan. On one of these, prompted, perhaps, by the fear of the unpromising political conditions he had left behind him, he did not return to American soil.

A former and more brief presentation by me of this hypothesis has since received affirmation of a rather surprising character. Professor J. Macmillan Brown, in his *Riddle of the Pacific*, a work already alluded to, and published some nine months later than mine, supplies an extraordinary analogy drawn from the mythology of Easter Island. Thus, two independent workers have discovered illustrations of fertility myths of similar character in connection with sunken areas.

Professor Brown's conclusions regarding Easter Island, the myths and customs of which he has studied closely, are that it was formerly the centre of a vast Pacific archipelagic civilisation of Polynesian origin, and that its present isolated position is due to the fact that the archipelago of which it was formerly a part underwent submergence. From the collected legends of the island he describes how Hotu Matua, the culture-hero, the Quetzalcoatl of this submerged empire, marooned on Easter Island with a small band of civilised followers, set himself to the task of reconstructing society on his restricted retreat.

" Assuming," says Professor Brown, " that the island was full of toilers at the great works of art, subjects of the powers in the archipelagoes and dependent on them for organisation and sustenance, we can imagine what a chaos it would be when the source of authority and of food had gone down ; we can imagine what a task lay in front of Hotu Matua, the only representative of the vanished government. What could he do with his three hundred against the thousands who felt that their chains were broken, and that if organised and led they could do what they liked with the island and the officials of their old masters ? "

Consequently Hotu Matua " set himself deliberately to assume the character and direct the old veneration of royalty towards himself " as the only remaining official of the submerged imperial government. He therefore developed the use of the Polynesian taboos to secure the influence of himself and his clan and descendants. The Miru or religion he inculcated was " an honoured name in the Polynesian fatherland amongst a lighter-coloured race." " No decree or command of his was efficient without some taboo," and these taboos extended to marriage and food. He also inculcated the idea that his head possessed a marvellous fertilising power. " If it came near any crop it would double or treble the growth." But what if he or his descendants fell into senility or decay ? " To prevent this he arranged that when the eldest son of a king married, his father should resign and retire into private life."

Now Quetzalcoatl was faced with practically the same conditions. He and his band of nobles must assert themselves or perish in the strange land which they had been compelled to seek by reason of the submergence, total or partial, of their fatherland. Like Hotu Matua, he set himself the task of strengthening the ancient religion. That

the pontificate of this faith was sedulously handed down
from father to son is shown by the careful provisions
effected to ensure this by the Zapotec priests of Quetzalcoatl at Mitla, one of the earliest localities where his religion
took root. These, when an heir was needed, reduced their
high priest to a state of intoxication, and presented him
with a noble virgin, with whose assistance he carried on
the divine line. Certain foods and beverages, too, both in
Mexico and Central America, were inalienable from the
royal and priestly caste. Like Hotu Matua, Quetzalcoatl
founded a special caste, the Votanides. The fertilising
power of the head of Quetzalcoatl is also to be observed
in the symbol for maize, in which the plant is seen growing
out of the head of the Maya god Ghanan, who is probably
a surrogate of Quetzalcoatl. Moreover, as in the case of
Hotu Matua, there was scarcely a single cultural or social
custom among the Maya which was not either held to have
been organised by Quetzalcoatl or in some manner referred
to him.

Thus the circumstances of the legends of Hotu Matua
and Quetzalcoatl are analogous, and we see that two
culture-heroes, both emanating from submerged localities,
evolved very similar religious ideas, and a similar social
system under pressure of like circumstances.

Summarising the evidence adduced in this chapter, we
find :

(1) That the Toltecs were an actual historical people
who arrived in Mexico at some time in the seventh
century A.D.

(2) That the tradition of the destruction of their city
of Tollan is probably a reminiscence of, or in some manner
became confused with, that of the destruction of Atlantis.

(8) That Quetzalcoatl, their first king, was an historical
personage, and the leader of a migration from Antillia.
He was also regarded as the leader of the Maya migration,
which reached Central America eight centuries before the
settlement of the Toltecs in Mexico. This implies that
the myth was brought to Mexico by Maya-Toltecs, who
naturalised it there.

(4) That a tradition similar to that of Quetzalcoatl is
associated with Easter Island in the Pacific, in a region
known once to have been occupied by land now submerged.

CHAPTER IV

ATLANTIS IN AMERICAN TRADITION

IF there be any justification for the theory that Atlantean influence penetrated to American soil, its remains should surely be manifest in the myths, tales and traditions of the Indian races which inhabit the continent. Do these exhibit traces of the Atlantean story, and do such fragmentary memories find their counterparts in the Platonic description of Atlantis, in the circumstances of its civilisation and its destruction ? Assuredly they do. Let us examine those American myths and legends which reveal Atlantean connections.

And first those which seem to preserve a more or less fragmentary memory of certain circumstances alluded to in Plato's account. In his *Critias* Plato tells us that the gods, dividing the regions of the earth among themselves, apportioned the island of Atlantis to Poseidon or Neptune. On that side of it which overlooked the sea was a fertile plain, at a distance of fifty stadia, from which rose a low mountain inhabited by a native of the country, Evenor, along with his wife Leucippe and his daughter Cleito. Poseidon fell in love with the maiden, and so that no man might reach her, he enclosed the hill where she dwelt with alternate zones of sea and land. In this enclosure he begat five pairs of twin boys, among whom he divided the island. Of these the eldest was Atlas, who retained the paramount power, the others being rulers of neighbouring islands. The later Atlanteans built on the summit of the hill a temple dedicated to Poseidon and Cleito, surrounded by a golden enclosure, containing golden statues of Poseidon, his wife and ten sons.

The Creek Indians, the Choctaws and Seminoles, preserve a myth which has more than a superficial resemblance to the above. They say that when the earth rose out of the waste of waters a great hill known as Nunne Chaha stood in the midst, and in the centre of it was the house of Esaugetuh Emissee, " The Master of Breath." He formed men from clay and erected a great encircling wall, upon which he placed the clay men to dry. He then took upon himself the task of directing the waters into channels, reserving the dry land for the men he had created.

Manibozho, the great god of the Algonquin Indians, is

said to have " carved the land and sea to his liking," just as the Huron deity Tawiscara " guided the waters into smooth channels." The Peruvian god Pariacaca arrived, as Poseidon had done, in a hilly country. But the people reviled him, and he sent a great flood upon them, so that their village was destroyed. Meeting a beautiful maiden, Choque Suso, who was weeping bitterly, he inquired the cause of her grief, and she informed him that the maize crop was dying for lack of water. He assured her that he would revive the maize if she would bestow her affections on him, and when she consented to his suit, he irrigated the land by canals. Eventually he turned his wife into a statue.

Another Peruvian myth recounts that the god Thonapa, angered at the people of Yamquisapa in the province of Alla-suyu because they were so bent on pleasure, drowned their city in a great lake. The people of this region worshipped a statue in the form of a woman which stood on the summit of the hill Cachapucara. Thonapa destroyed both hill and image and disappeared into the sea.

Here we have what students of Folklore call " the test of recurrence." These Peruvian myths have a close agreement with the details of Plato's account which deal with the wooing of Cleito and the enclosure of the hill and the making of an irrigation zone. Here, too, we find mention in one case of a statue of the wife of the god, while in the other the statue is alluded to, and the deity is described as disappearing into the sea. As in Plato's *Critias*, the flood was precipitated by the wickedness or love of pleasure of the human race.

So much then for the fact that we discover what seem to be definite fragments in American myth of that part of the Atlantean tradition which related to the settlement of Poseidon in the island-continent. Let us now examine the legends of the New World which describe earthquakes or great cataclysms of nature, such as Plato tells us overtook Atlantis, and see whether such as we find appear in any way to corroborate the Platonic account. Atlantis, Plato tells us, disappeared beneath the sea after a visitation of earthquake and flood.

We find, perhaps, the most striking analogy in that ancient book of the Quiche Indians of Guatemala known as the Popol Vuh. For generations antiquaries interested in the past of Central America believed that this wonderful compilation existed somewhere in Guatemala. They were aware that a certain Don Felix Cabrera had made use of it early in the nineteenth century, but the whereabouts of the copy he had seen could not be discovered. Dr. C. Scherzer, an Austrian scholar, resolved to trace it if possible, and proceeded to Guatemala in 1854 for this purpose. After a diligent search he succeeded in finding the lost manuscript in the University of San Carlos in the city of Guatemala, where it had been conveyed from the library of a convent in 1830.[1]

The name " Popol Vuh " means " The Collection of Written Leaves," which in itself shows that the book must have been reduced to writing at an early period. It is, indeed, a traditional and historical compilation. The language in which it was written is the Quiche, a dialect of the Maya, still spoken in Guatemala and San Salvador.

The beginning of this interesting book is occupied with the story of the creation, and what occurred subsequently to that event. Experimenting in the making of human beings, the gods created mannikins of wood. But these were irreverent and moved them to wrath. The deities resolved to destroy them, and Hurakan, the Heart of Heaven, caused the waters to be swollen so that a mighty flood came upon the mannikins. A thick resinous rain was cast down upon them. The bird Xecotcovatch tore out their eyes, the bird Camulatz cut off their heads, the bird Cotzbalam devoured their flesh, the bird Tecumbalam broke their bones and sinews and ground them into powder. Then all sorts of beings great and small abused the mannikins. The household utensils and domestic animals jeered at them and made game of them in their plight. In their despair the unfortunate mannikins ran hither and thither. They mounted upon the roofs of the houses, but the houses crumbled beneath their feet. They tried to climb to the tops of the trees, but the trees hurled them down. Even the caves closed before them. Thus this ill-starred race was finally destroyed and overthrown, and " the only vestiges of them which remain are certain of their progeny, the little monkeys which dwell in the woods."

[1] See my essay, *The Popol Vuh*, London, 1908.

It does not appear to me to be possible for a tradition so striking as the above to have originated otherwise than out of a very powerful and persistent folk-memory of cataclysm and catastrophe. We have here a vivid description of the approach of a mighty flood, the descent of a fiery volcanic rain, the destruction of dwellings, the crashing of trees, and the ultimate plight of the wretched survivors, reduced to the condition of forest-dwellers. I believe the Popol Vuh to contain a residuum of tradition neither American nor European, but Atlantean.

Many of the legends of the South American tribes recount similar disasters. The Tupi-Guarani of Brazil have a tradition of cataclysm almost as striking as that detailed in the Popol Vuh. Says Thevet, who collected their myths : " Monan, the Maker, the Begetter, without beginning or end, author of all that is, seeing the ingratitude of men and their contempt for him that had made them thus joyous, withdrew from them, and sent upon them *tata*, the divine fire, which burned all that was on the surface of the earth. He swept about the fire in such a way that in places he raised mountains and in others deep valleys. Of all men, one alone, Irin Magé (the One who Sees), was saved, whom Monan carried into the heaven. He, seeing all things destroyed, spoke thus to Monan : ' Wilt thou also destroy all the heavens and their garniture ? Alas ! henceforth where will be our home ? Why should I live, since there is none other of my kind ? ' Then Monan was so filled with pity that he poured a deluging rain on the earth, which quenched the fire, and flowing from all sides, formed the ocean which we call *partana*, the great waters."

The Guaymis of Costa Rica, a tribe with South American affinities, told the story thus : " Angered with the world, the mighty Noncomala poured over it a flood of water, killing every man and woman. But the kindly god Nubu had preserved the seed of a man, and when the waters had dried up he sowed it upon the moist earth. From the best of it rose the race of men, and from that which was imperfect came the monkeys."[1]

To summarise other striking American myths of cataclysm : The Algonquin Indians told how Manibozho, their god, was once engaged in hunting, when the wolves he

[1] Melendez, *Tesoros Verdaderos de las Yndias*, I, p. 4.

used as dogs entered a lake and disappeared. He followed them into its depths, but it suddenly overflowed and submerged the entire world. The god, desirous of reconstructing the earth, dispatched a raven to seek for a piece of soil, but it returned without fulfilling its mission. In the end the musk-rat succeeded in obtaining sufficient earth to recreate the terrestrial sphere.

An Arawak legend told how the Great Spirit, Aimon Kondi, scourged the world by fire, from which the survivors sought refuge in caverns. A great flood followed, in which Marerewana and his followers saved themselves in a canoe.[1] A Carib deluge myth tells how an extraordinary rainfall precipitated a great flood, from which mankind was saved by the ibis, which scraped up sufficient earth with its beak to form the dry land and the mountains. The Muyscas of Bogota attributed the deluge to the overflowing of a lake through the spite or treachery of Chia, the moon goddess. The flood-myth of the Karaya of Brazil relates that the malevolent agency Anatiwa originated the deluge, and sent fish to pull down those who had taken flight to the hill Tupimare.

On the subject of the American tradition of a deluge Brinton says : " How familiar such speculations were to the aborigines of America there is abundance evidence to show. The early Algonkin legends do not speak of an antediluvian race, nor any family who escaped the waters. . . . Nor did their neighbours, the Dakotas, though firm in the belief that the globe had once been destroyed by the waters, suppose that any had escaped. The same view was entertained by the Nicaraguas and the Botocudos of Brazil. . . . The Aschochimi of California told of the drowning of the world so that no man escaped. . . . Much

---

[1] W. H. Brett, *Indian Tribes of Guiana*, p. 378 ff. Brinton in a valuable note to a series of flood myths in his *Myths of the New World* (p. 245), remarks : " The American nations among whom a distinct and well-authenticated myth of the deluge was found are the Athapascas, Algonkins, Iroquois, Cherokees, Chicasaws, Caddos, Caraxas, Guaymis, Pumarys, Pawnees, Natchas, Dakotas, Apaches, Navahoes, Mandans, Pueblo Indians, Aztecs, Mixtecs, Zapotecs, Tlascalans, Mechoacans, Toltecs, Nahuas, Maya, Quiches, Haitians, natives of Darien and Popoyan, Muyscas, Quichuas, Tupinambas, Achaguas, Araucanians and many others. . . . Andree's Fluthsagen quotes a number." I have quoted American flood myths extensively in my *Dictionary of Non-Classical Mythology*, pp. 42–54.

the most general opinion, however, was that some few escaped the desolating element . . . by ascending some mountain, on a raft or canoe, in a cave, or even by climbing a tree. No doubt some of these legends have been modified by Christian teachings, but many of them are so connected with local peculiarities and ancient religious ceremonies that no unbiassed student can assign them wholly to that source. . . . There are no more common heirlooms in the traditional lore of the red race. Nearly every old author quotes one or more of them. They present great uniformity of outline, and rather than engage in repetitions of little interest they can more profitably be studied in the aggregate than in detail. By far the greater number represent the last destruction of the world to have been by water. A few, however . . . attribute it to a general conflagration which swept over the earth, consuming every living thing except a few who took refuge in a deep cave. . . . There are, indeed, some points of striking similarity between the deluge myths of Asia and America. It has been called a peculiarity of the latter that in them the person saved is always the first man. This, though not without exception, is certainly the general rule. But these first men were usually the highest deities known to their nations, the only creators of the world, and the guardians of the race." They were, in fact, such figures as Poseidon and his son Atlas.

The Codex Chimalpopoca, a work in the ancient Nahuatl language of Mexico, written about half a century after the Conquest, contains the following flood myth :

" And this year was that of Ce-calli, and on the first day all was lost. The mountain itself was submerged in the water, and the water itself remained tranquil for fifty-two springs. Now towards the close of the year Titlacahuan had forewarned the man named Nata and his wife named Nena, saying, ' Make no more pulque, but straightway hollow out a large cypress, and enter it when in the month Tozoztli the water shall approach the sky.' They entered it, and when Titlacahuan had closed the door he said, ' Thou shalt eat but a single ear of maize, and thy wife but one also.'

" As soon as they had finished eating they went forth and the water was tranquil, for the log did not move any more, and opening it, they saw many fish. Then they built a fire, rubbing together pieces of wood, and they roasted the fish. The gods Citlallinicue and Citlallatonac, looking down below, exclaimed, ' Divine Lord, what means that fire below ? Why do they thus smoke the heavens ? '

" Straightway descended Titlacahuan Tezcatlipoca and commenced to rate them, saying, ' What is this fire doing here ? ' And seizing the fishes, he moulded their hinder parts and changed their heads, and they were at once transformed into dogs."

This curious myth is more than a mere account of flood, for it illustrates a new type of sacrifice on the part of the Mexican people, the change from the fish sacrifice or fish pabulum to the dog sacrifice or pabulum which is historically known to have taken place at some remote period when the Mexican tribes ceased to be a people dwelling on " a great water," and became an inland and agricultural folk. But it is only one of a number of extraordinary cataclysmic myths enshrined in the traditions of the Aztec and other Indian races of Mexico. The Aztecs believed that the earth had been destroyed on several occasions, by the agency of fire, tempest and water. They thought that the various " suns," as they called the epochs into which their traditional time-periods were divided, had each been terminated by some awful convulsion of nature. Humboldt suggested that these " suns " were " fictions of mythological astronomy, modified either by obscure reminiscences of some great revolution suffered by our planet, or by physical hypotheses, suggested by the sight of marine petrifactions and fossil remains." The Abbé Brasseur, in his works on ancient Mexico, interpreted them as exaggerated references to historical events.

The Mexicans believed that the earth was not destined to receive its present inhabitants, although occupied by man-like beings, until it had undergone a series of cataclysms or partial destructions, regarding the precise incidence and even the number of which there is a marked difference of opinion on the part of the older authorities. The interpreter of the Codex Vaticanus states that " in the first age " (or sun) " water reigned until at last it destroyed the world. . . . This age, according to their computation, lasted 4008 years, and on the occurrence of that great deluge they say that men were changed into fish named Tlacamichin, which signifies men-fish." The second age, he tells us, lasted for 4010 years, and the world was destroyed by the force of violent tempests, the catastrophe concluding by the transformation of men into monkeys. The third age endured for 4801 years, and ended in a universal fire, and in the fourth, which occupied 5042 years, the human race, which had never ceased to transmit a few survivors from one of these epochs to the next, was almost destroyed by famine.

The native historian Ixtlilxochitl in his *History of the Chichimecs* calls the first of these epochs Atonatiuh, or the Water Sun, because it was ended by a great inundation. The second epoch, Tlachitonatiuh, or Earth Sun, closed with violent earthquakes. In this age flourished the Quinames, or giants. The third epoch was Ecatonatiuh, or the " Wind Sun," in which houses, trees and men were nearly all destroyed by hurricanes, those who remained being changed into creatures of an intelligence so low as to be almost indistinguishable from monkeys. He does not furnish us with the name of the present age.

Another historian of Mexico, Camargo, seems to have been indebted to Ixtlilxochitl for his version of the creation myth, but he seems to have been under the impression that only two of the epochs were ended. That three past cataclysms had taken place and that four ages in all had occurred is, indeed, the most generally favoured version of the story, but some authorities seem to have been of the opinion that a myth was current among the Mexican people which stated that no less than five epochs had taken place in the history of the world. Gama, Gomara and Humboldt share this view, while Mendieta held that the Aztecs believed in the existence of five past suns.

It is probable, however, that this cataclysmic theory was in vogue among the Nahua peoples for generations before it received a more or less definite " literary " form, and indeed Veytia and Ixtlilxochitl both state that the number of suns was agreed upon at a meeting of native astronomers within traditional memory. We are probably following the official version of the myth if we accept that to which the so-called Calendar Stone of Mexico, now in the Museo Naçional in Mexico City, gives sculptured form, and which may be interpreted as follows : While the world was wrapped in primeval gloom, the god Tezcatlipoca transformed himself into the sun. This epoch, which was known as " Four Jaguar," ended in the destruction of humanity and the race of giants who then inhabited the world by fierce jaguars. The god Quetzalcoatl became the second sun, and the age of " Four Wind " ended in violent hurricanes, during which men were transformed into monkeys. The god Tlaloc then took upon himself the task of providing the world with light, and his epoch of " Four Rain " came to an end by means of a deluge of fire. The goddess Chalchihuitlicue represented the sun of the age of " Four Water," at the end of which there descended a deluge in which men were changed into fishes. Later appeared the present sun, "Four Motions," which, it was believed, would terminate in earthquakes.

One of the flood myths of Mexico has a close resemblance to the Biblical account of the fall of the Tower of Babel. The story is to be found in the Codex Vaticanus. " In this first age," it says, " giants existed in that country (Mexico). They relate of one of the seven whom they mention as having escaped from the deluge that, the earth becoming populous, he went to Cholula, and there began to build a tower which is that of which the brick base is still visible. The name of that chief was Xelhua. He built it in order that should a deluge come again he might escape to it. Its base is 1800 feet in circumference. When it had already reached a great height lightning from heaven fell and destroyed it. Those Indians who were under that chief who had escaped from the deluge, named Xelhua, made bricks out of a mountain in Tlalmanalco called Cocotle, and from Tlalmanalco to Cholula Indians were placed to pass the bricks from hand to hand. And thus they built this tower that was named Tulan Cholula, which was so high that it appeared to reach heaven. And being content, since it seemed to them that they had a place to escape from the deluge if it should again happen, and from which they might ascend into heaven, a Chalchiuitl, which is a precious stone, fell from thence and struck it to the ground. Others say that the Chalchiuitl was in the shape of a toad, and that whilst destroying the tower it reprimanded them, inquiring of them their reason for wishing to ascend into heaven, since it was sufficient for them to see what was on the earth."

In passing, I may observe that this myth, in common with several other legends already described, alludes to a sacred hill, as does that in Plato's *Critias,* and it is to be noted that, like the story of Plato, it refers to the race of Titans or giants who occupied the earth in early times.

The Mixtecs, a highly civilised race dwelling in South-western Mexico, had a tradition of flood which appears to me to enshrine Atlantean reminiscences. It tells us that " In the day of obscurity and darkness, when there were as yet no days nor years, the world was a chaos sunk in darkness, while the earth was covered with water on which slime and scum floated. One day the deer-god and goddess appeared. They had human form, and out of their magic they raised a great mountain out of the water and built on it beautiful palaces for their dwelling. These buildings stood in Upper Mixteca, close to the place Apoala (Accu-mulation of Water) and the mountain which was called ' Place Where the Heavens Stood.' " These deities had twin sons, and all four were skilled in magic. "The deer-gods had more sons and daughters, but there came a flood in which many of these perished. After the catastrophe was over the god who is called the creator of all things formed the heavens and earth and restored the human race."

Here once again we encounter the mountain, the twins, the " accumulation of water " or canals, and the male and female deity dwelling in an enclosed place in undisturbed peace, as did Poseidon and Cleito. It is significant that the deities mentioned in the Mixtec myth were deer-gods, for the deer in Mexico is the symbol of water.

In the preface to his *Creation Myths of Primitive America,* Mr. Jeremiah Curtin includes a tradition the importance of which, from the viewpoint of the student of the Atlantean theory, demands quotation.

" The creation myths of America," he says, " form a complete system. They give a detailed and circumstantial account of the origin of this world and of all things and creatures contained in it. In the course of the various narratives which compose this myth system *an earlier world is described to us, with an order of existence and a method of conduct on which the life of primitive man in America was patterned.*

" That earlier world had two periods of duration—one of complete and perfect harmony ; another of violence, collision and conflict. . . . Described briefly and by an Indian, the American myth system is as follows : ' There was a world before this one in which we are living at present. That was the world of the first people, who were different from us altogether. Those people were very numerous, so numerous that if a count could be made of all the stars in the sky, all the feathers on birds, all the hair and fur on animals they would not be so numerous as the first people.

" ' These people lived very long in peace, in concord, in harmony, in happiness. No man knows, no man can tell, how long they lived in that way. At last the minds of all except a very small number were changed. They fell into conflict—one offended another, consciously or unconsciously, one injured another with or without intention, one wanted some special thing, another wanted that very thing also. Conflict set in, and because of this came a time of activity and struggle, to which there was no end or stop till the great majority of the first people—that is all except a small number—were turned into the various kinds of living creatures that are on earth now or have ever been on earth, except man—that is, all kinds of beasts, birds, reptiles, fish, worms and insects, as well as trees, plants, grasses, rocks and some mountains. They were turned into everything that we see on the earth or in the sky.

" ' The small number of the former people who did not quarrel, those great first people of the old time who remained of one mind and harmonious, left the earth, *sailed away westward*, passed that line where the sky comes down to the earth and touches it, sailed to places beyond ; stayed there or withdrew to upper regions and lived in them happily, lived in agreement, live so to-day, and will live in the same way hereafter.' "

This description of the ancient world by an Indian

might well have been drawn from Plato's account of Atlantis. It speaks of a teeming and civilised country which must have been situated in the ocean and east of America, as its survivors " sailed away westward " from its shores. It describes almost exactly the alteration in the mental attitude of the people of Atlantis of which Plato speaks. He says that for generations the polity of the first divine Atlanteans, the civilisers, remained undisturbed. The people were gentle and obedient to the laws and to the gods, and wise and charitable in their intercourse with one another. But gradually the blood of the gods which flowed in their veins became diluted with the mortal admixture, and they grew degenerate, so that Zeus regarded them with disfavour. The native Indian whom Curtin quotes says that these " first people " were " different from us altogether." " They lived long in peace, in concord and in happiness," for " no man knows how long." At last " their minds were changed." Only a few retained the ancient worthiness. They offended each other. They became like animals in their selfishness and their desires.

But the worthy remnant, " those great first people of the old time who remained of one mind and harmonious," the civilised few who jealously retained the tradition of culture and propriety, " sailed away westward . . . to places beyond."

If the above is not a true reminiscence of the Atlantis myth, I am much at fault. To be sure, the final catastrophe is not alluded to. But is it not mentioned in other accounts, as we have seen ? This naïf Indian story speaks of unrest and rebellion and the final break-up of a social system. It is at such a crisis that Plato's account of the affairs of Atlantis breaks off short. Zeus is about to rebuke the Atlanteans. After that we know nothing. But that a certain number left Atlantis after the final catastrophe is one of the most certain things in tradition.

Let us examine the possible relationship of these American myths to the Atlantean tradition a little more closely. As the annexed table shows, the " test of recurrence," as it is called by students of Folklore, is readily observed in those of them which resemble the account of Plato, or at least its first part, in their general circumstances.

	Sacred Hill.	Zone-making.	God and maiden.	Twins.	Sacred imago.	Flood.
Plato's Myth	,,	,,	,,	,,	,,	,,
Creek Myth	,,	,,				
Peruvian (1)		,,	,,		,,	,,
Peruvian (2)	,,				,,	,,

In the Creek legend we find mention both of the sacred hill and the zones of land and water alluded to in Plato's account. In the first Peruvian example we have the zones, or their equivalent, the amour of a god with a maiden, the image of the beloved set up as a statue or idol, and the flood, this account omitting the episodes of the sacred hill and the twin offspring only. The second Peruvian example gives us the hill, the image and the flood, but omits the other three episodes. The recurrence of the Atlantean myth in America is thus clear enough, for every episode of its first portion reappears in one or other of these tales, save that relating to the twin offspring. It may be remarked in passing, however, that sacred twins are more commonly encountered in American mythology than in any other.

The late Sir George Lawrence Gomme was among the first to show that if one part of a myth were found in one part of the world and another section of it in another part, that these were demonstrably floating portions of a formerly homogeneous myth, and were supplementary to each other. He demonstrated that if we possessed the original myth—as we happily do in this case—and could build up its parts from scattered fragments, that that original must formerly have had a wide acceptance. He also made it clear that if a myth had no significance of itself, but could be proved to fit in with the details of another myth, that it must be a missing portion of it.[1] It seems to me that from the examples I have adduced in these pages one can say without dubiety that the circumstances of Plato's myth are clearly duplicated and supplemented.

But we must now turn to those American myths which reveal a close connection with other Atlantean traditions. We find the Greek myth of Atlas duplicated in America.

---

[1] See his *Ethnology in Folklore, passim.*

Atlas, the Greek story says, supported the world on his shoulders. The Mundruku Indians of Brazil have a myth which tells how a god Raimi made the world and placed it in the shape of a flat stone on the head of another god. The Muyscas of Colombia say that Bochica or Nemqueteba, the god of day, like another Atlas bore the earth upon his shoulders.

A myth found in the eloquent pages of Ovid is duplicated in American tradition. The tale in question is that of Deucalion, the son of Prometheus the Titan, who has been connected by certain writers with Atlantis. According to Lucian, Deucalion was the Noah of the Greek world. " I have heard in Greece," says Lucian, " what the Greeks say of Deucalion. The present race of men, they allege, is not the first, for they totally perished, but a second generation, who, being descended from Deucalion, increased to a great multitude. Of those former men they thus speak—they were insolent and addicted to unjust actions ; they neither regarded oaths, nor were they hospitable to strangers, nor listened to suppliants ; and this complicated wickedness was the cause of their destruction. On a sudden the earth poured forth a vast quantity of water, great rains fell, the rivers overflowed, and the sea rose to a prodigious height. All things became water, and all men were destroyed. Only Deucalion was left, for a second race of men, on account of his prudence and piety. He was saved in this manner. He went into a large ark or chest, and when he was within, there entered swine, horses, lions, serpents, and all other creatures which live on earth, by pairs. He received them all, and they did him no hurt, for the gods created a friendship among them, so that they all sailed in one chest whilst the waters prevailed."

To discover what occurred when they had subsided we must return to Ovid. He tells us that Deucalion and his wife Pyrrha escaped the flood in " a little barque," and that when they gained the shore Deucalion turned to his wife Pyrrha and addressed her in what, considering all the circumstances, seems rather a lengthy speech.

" They agree to address the heavenly powers in pious prayers and seek relief from the sacred oracles. They repair, therefore, without delay to the banks of Cephisus, whose waters, though troubled, were yet gliding along their wonted channel, and directed their steps toward the temple of the sacred goddess.

"She was softened by their pious prayers, and thus graciously answered : ' Depart from the temple, veil your heads, and loosening your garments, throw behind you the bones of your mighty mother.' Long they stood amazed, till Pyrrha first breaks silence and refuses to obey the dire commands of the goddess. . . . At length the son of Prometheus thus, with mild benevolence, addresses his spouse : ' Either my discernment fails or the oracles are just, and advise no sacrilege. Our mighty mother is the earth, and the stones in the body of the earth are, as I imagine, called her bones. These we are commanded to throw behind us.' Pyrrha, though pleased with the solution of her spouse, yet fluctuates between hope and fear, so much do both distrust the commands of heaven. But where is the harm to make the attempt ? They descend from the mount, veil their heads, unbind their veils, and, as commanded, throw stones behind them. The stones (who could believe it, did not antiquity bear witness to the tradition ?) began to lay aside their hardness and natural rigour, and, softening by degrees, to assume a new shape—the forms of men and women."

I have quoted from this myth directly, because it has been so frequently alluded to in Atlantean literature with scant reference to its actual terms, and for the more pressing reason that it has its precise counterparts in American myth. Humboldt informs us that the Tamanacs, a Central American tribe, believe that in the great deluge a man and a woman saved themselves on a high mountain called Tamanacu, and casting behind them and over their heads the fruits of the Mauritius palm tree, the seeds in these produced men and women. The Macusi tribe of the Arawak Indians believed that the one man who survived the deluge replenished the earth by changing stones into human beings.

It is thus very plain indeed that the whole circumstances, not only of the original Atlantean myth but of its affluents as well, are reproduced in America, where almost absolute identity with their terms is encountered. That such identity cannot be fortuitous is obvious. I shall return later to this subject when I come to deal with the resemblances between those mythological figures of the Old and New Worlds which have a bearing on Atlantean tradition, but for the present I believe that I have adduced sufficient evidence for the appearance of the Atlantean tradition on American soil to uphold the general hypothesis I have advanced.

CHAPTER V

THE ATLANTEAN TRADITION IN AMERICAN RELIGION

WE have seen that the myths and traditions of America preserve a very definite memory of Atlantis and of the great upheavals which culminated in its destruction. What we must now ask is : do the religious ideas of America and the god-like figures round which they cluster show any resemblance to what we know of Atlantean religion or any connection with its tradition ?

The principal mythological figures alluded to in Plato's story of Atlantis are Poseidon, Cleito and Atlas. As regards the Atlantean religion, Plato informs us that in the centre of the city was a temple dedicated to Cleito and Poseidon, surrounded by a golden enclosure. He also observes that a religion seems to have centred round the rite of bull sacrifice.

The figure of Poseidon is too well known to require much description. Among the Greeks he was the god of the sea, who lived in the depths of the ocean, and he had an added significance as lord of the earthquake and all subterranean disturbance. Do we encounter in the religions of America any divine figures approaching closely to this conception ?

As has already been said, those ancient deities of the ocean, the Gucumatz, alluded to in the Popol Vuh, closely resemble this marine and earthquake deity. In that work they are alluded to as " the old serpents covered with green and blue feathers (or scales) who live in the depths of the ocean." These are associated with Quetzalcoatl, whose parents they seem to have been. He was indeed one of the Gucumatz or marine deities, and was closely connected with water, and it was these Gucumatz or Old Ones who brought floods and disaster on the first men mentioned in the Popol Vuh.

Another Mexican god, Tlaloc, the god of water, closely resembles Poseidon. He appears to have a head evolved from that of a walrus, with large tusks, and an early sculpture shows, I think, the process of development from that form. He possessed, like Poseidon, both beneficent and terrible aspects, and was the striker and the slayer, as well as the god of all moisture and the sea. Sometimes he is depicted as a monstrous serpent or dragon, as in page 74 of the Maya Dresden Codex, vomiting forth water upon the earth. In an ancient hymn addressed to him, he is alluded to as having come out of " the Tlalocan, the blue house," that is, the sea. According to Boturini, quoting Gemelli Carreri (tom. 6, p. 83), Tlaloc was the deity who at the behest of Tezcatlipoca raised the earth out of the waters of the universal flood, and who counsels men by

Mexican deity Tlaloc in walrus form from
Castillo de Teayo, Mexico.

his divine messages, written in the lightning and the thunderbolt, to live wisely and morally. He was also known as the Pearl Serpent, a name frequently given in mythology to the dragons which haunt the depths of the sea.

Just as the Greek gods divided the world among themselves and the sea fell to the lot of Poseidon, as Plato tells us, so did the sea-god of Peru apportion the world among his three sons. To Viracocha was given the rule of the sea. The Aymara-Quichua race worshipped Viracocha as a great culture hero. They did not offer him sacrifices or tribute, as they thought that he, being creator and possessor of all things, needed nothing from men, so they only gave him worship. After him they idolised the sun. They believed, indeed, that Viracocha had both made sun and moon, after emerging from Lake Titicaca, and that then he made the earth and peopled it. On his travels westward from the lake he was sometimes assailed by men, but he revenged himself by sending terrible storms upon them and destroying their property, so they humbled themselves and acknowledged him as their lord. He forgave them and taught them everything, obtaining from them the name of Pachayachachic. In the end he disappeared in the western ocean.

I have before mentioned the circumstance that Quetzalcoatl, the son of the Gucumatz, who resembled Poseidon, is himself very similar to Atlas the son of Poseidon. Both are twins, are bearded, and both are represented as bearing the world on their heads. Both also are mentioned as having their place of abode on the summit of a mountain, and there are still other points of resemblance between them.

We will observe, too, that Cleito, the beloved of Poseidon, is connected with irrigation. Her statue or idol was represented in the temple of Poseidon on a sacred hill at Atlantis. This looks to me as if she were one of those deities associated with the fertility of the earth. America, and especially Mexico, is rich in such deities. There is a distinct group of these, which clusters round the goddess Coatlicue. Now much as I dislike etymological comparisons, this name seems to me to present a curious resemblance to that of Cleito, just as the syllable Uitzil in the name of Uitzilopochtli, the Mexican war-god, seems to me a reminiscence of Atlas. At least it is strange enough to find deities possessing names and myths so curiously similar. Let us summarise the resemblance in a few lines.

Cleito, the spouse of Poseidon, is connected with irrigation. Her idol was worshipped in Atlantis on a sacred mountain or hill.

Coatlicue was the personification of a mountain near Tollan, the streams of which flowed down to irrigate the fields. She was the mother of the war-god Uitzilopochtli, by Mixcoatl, the god of the thunder-cloud.

Atlas is the twin son of Cleito, and supports the world on his back.

Uitzilopochtli, the son of Coatlicue, is also shown supporting the world on his back, or as one of the world-bearers. In some myths he is spoken of as the twin of Quetzalcoatl, who likewise is a world- or heaven-bearer.

Moreover, the worship of all these deities was connected with mountains. However these parallels may commend themselves to others, they appear to me as very clear. Nor are there mythological resemblances to them elsewhere. The complex of the mountain, the mother and the twin son is not to be paralleled in the world's mythology, so far as I am aware.

We must also consider the last phase of Atlantean worship—the cult of the twin, for that twins were worshipped in Atlantis is clear from the fact that the idols of Poseidon's ten twin sons were associated with those of himself and his wife in the temple ritual. Now if there is one region of the world more than any other in which the cult of the twin is universal, it is America. The cult is certainly to be encountered elsewhere, but nowhere is it so commonly found as on American soil. In Peru the statue of the god Apocatequil was erected on the mountains with that of his mother on one hand and his twin brother on the other. In memory of these brothers, twins in Peru were deemed sacred to the lightning, and when a woman or even a llama brought them forth, a fast was held and sacrifices offered to the two pristine brothers, with a chant commencing " O thou who causest twins." Brebeuf, a Jesuit missionary who resided among the Hurons in 1626, states that they possessed two gods—Joskeha and Tawiscara, twin-born of a virgin mother. Brinton says: " The brothers quarrelled, and finally came to blows ; the former using the horns of a stag, the latter the wild rose. He of the weaker weapon was very naturally discomfited and sorely wounded. Fleeing for life, the blood gushed from him at every step, and as it fell turned into flint-stones. The victor returned to his grandmother, and established his lodge in the far east, on the borders of the great ocean, whence the sun comes. In time he became the father of mankind, and special guardian of the Iroquois.

" The earth was at first arid and sterile, but he destroyed the gigantic frog which had swallowed all the waters, and guided the torrents into smooth streams and lakes. The woods he stocked with game ; and having learned from the great tortoise, who supports the world, how to make fire, taught his children, the Indians, this indispensable art. He it was who watched and watered their crops ; and, indeed, without his aid, says the old missionary, quite out of patience with these puerilities, ' they think they could not boil a pot.' Sometimes they spoke of him as the sun, but this only figuratively. . . .

" Both these heroes, let it be observed, live in the utter-most east ; both are the mythical fathers of the race. To the east, therefore, should these nations have pointed as their original dwelling-place. This they did, in spite of history. Cusic (a Tuscarora chief), who takes up the story of the Iroquois a thousand years before the Christian era, locates them first in the most eastern region they ever possessed, while the Algonkins with one voice called those of their tribes living nearest the rising sun *Abnakis*, ' our ancestors at the east,' or at the dawn ; literally ' our *white* ancestors.' "[1]

The creation myth of the Guaymis of Costa Rica related that the mysterious being Noncomala formed the world and the waters, but they were in darkness and clouds. Wading into the river, he met and fecundated the water-sprite Rutbe, who bore him twins, brothers, who lived and throve with their mother for twelve years. Then they left her, one becoming the sun, the other the moon, the twin lights of the world. In Central America twins were slain from religious motives.

Hun-Apu and Xbalanque, the hero-gods of the Popol Vuh, were twins, and appear to me clearly to resemble the Mexican gods Tezcatlipoca and Uitzilopochtli, who, like them, made a journey through the Country of the Dead. These deities are chiefs of the stars of the Northern and Southern hemispheres respectively, and in this they resemble the divinities of a curious European cult which has long been suspect of an Atlantean connection. This was the cult of the heavenly twins, the Cabiri, the first recorded mystery-cult in history.

What precisely was this cult of the Cabiri ? It is by no means easy to disentangle its significance from the enor-mous mass of detail concerning it in the writings of the

[1] *Myths of the New World*, p. 202 ff.

ancient mystics of the classical age. But as I am convinced that it has a real bearing on the question of Atlantean origins, I shall examine it briefly here, believing, too, that it throws light on the Atlantean connection of the twin cult in America.

Pherecides, Herodotus and Nonnus speak of the Cabiri as sons of Vulcan, Cicero calls them sons of Proserpine, and Jupiter is often named as their father. Dionysius of Halicarnassus, Macrobius, Varro and others consider them the same as the Penates of the Romans, in which, however, the Venetian Altori is opposed to them. According to his opinion and that of Vossius, the Cabiri were nothing more than the ministers of the gods, who were deified after their death, and the Dactyli, the Curetes, and the Corybantes were other names by which they were known. Strabo regards them as the ministers of Hecate. Bochart recognises in them the three principal infernal deities, Pluto, Proserpine and Mercury.

The worship of the Cabiri, if the general belief is to be credited, was originally derived from Egypt, where we find the ancient temple of Memphis consecrated to them. Herodotus supposes that the Pelasgians, the first inhabitants of the Peloponnessus, dwelt first in the isle of Samothrace, where they introduced this worship, and established the famous mysteries, into which such heroes as Cadmus, Orpheus, Hercules, Castor, Pollux, Ulysses, Agamemnon, Æneas and Philip, the father of Alexander, had the honour of being initiated. From their abode in Samothrace the Pelasgi carried these mysteries to Athens, whence they were conveyed to Thebes.

The Cabiri seem to have been worshipped at Memphis in a pigmy form, and are thus represented in the coins of Thessalonica, along with the insignia of Vulcan. They also appear in the mythology of the Phœnicians. In the isle of Lemnos and in Tenebros their mystic rites were celebrated. Authorities differ as regards their number, but it is generally accepted that they were twain. In later times they were identified with the twin Dioscuri, Castor and Pollux. Dionysius of Halicarnassus states that they were two " youths armed with spears."

Kenrick, a good authority, in his *Egypt before Herodotus*, stated that the countries in which the Samothracian and

Cabiriac worship prevailed were peopled either by the
Pelasgi or by the Æolians, who of all the tribes compre-
hended under the general name of Hellenes approach most
nearly in antiquity and language to the Pelasgi. " We
seem warranted, then," he says, " in two conclusions :
first, that the Pelasgian tribes in Italy, Greece and Asia
were united in times reaching high above the commencement of history by community of religious ideas and rites,
as well as letters, arts and language ; and secondly, that
large portions of what is called the heroic history of Greece,
are nothing else than fictions devised to account for the
traces of this affinity, when time and the ascendancy of
other nations had destroyed the primitive connection, and
rendered the cause of the similarity obscure. The original
derivation of the Cabiriac system from Phœnicia and
Egypt is a less certain, though still highly probable,
conclusion."

The name " Cabiri " has been very generally deduced
from the Phœnician " mighty," and this etymology is in
accordance with the fact that the gods of Samothrace were
called " Divi potes." Kenrick believed, however, that the
Phœnicians used some other name which the Greeks
translated " Kabeiros," and that it denoted the two
elements of fire and wind.

Sanconiathon, the Carthaginian writer, tells us that the
cult of the Cabiri was of Carthaginian origin, and was
associated with Osiris. The god Thoth ordained that the
Cabiri should set down their records of the past. The cult
of the Cabiri, indeed, appears to have been brought from
North Africa to Egypt and Greece, and it is expressly
stated that it was delivered among others to the Egyptian
Osiris. The Cabiri are said by Sanconiathon to have been
the inventors of boats, of the arts of hunting and fishing,
and of building and husbandry. They also invented the
art of writing, the use of salt and of medicines. Finally,
this writer tells us that Poseidon and the Cabiri were settled
at Berytus, but not till human sacrifice had been introduced. The Cabiri are in this passage alluded to as hus-
bandmen and fishermen, and the name in this connection
seems rather to apply to a race than to a cult.

I cannot cast aside the notion—for the lack of proof
does not permit that it should receive the name of theory—

that the myth of the Cabiri retains a tradition of the entry
into the Mediterranean area of a civilised race at a period
when that region was plunged in barbarism. We are informed that the cult of the Cabiri originated in Phœnicia.
It is much more likely that it originated in the new
Phœnicia that was Carthage than in the old that was Tyre.
If " Osiris " was one of its apostles, then it must have
come from North-west Africa, for it is clear that his
religion was carried to Egypt from that quarter. But we
cannot regard North-west Africa at any time in its history
as the home of a civilisation such as that which various
ancient authors attribute to the Cabirian cult or race.

The fact that they are mentioned as having been Pelasgians and the inventors of boats and as a race of fishermen
indicates, I think, that they were none other than those
Azilian-Tardenoisians who entered Europe some 8000 or
9000 years before our era, who were the prototypes of the
Iberian race, and, as I have said before, constituted the
last wave of immigrants from Atlantis. We have here a
race, the Cabiri, who suddenly invade Europe, bringing
with them a culture entirely alien to its rude peoples,
and whose origin is lost in the vague of antiquity. Is
it altogether unwise to associate it with the Azilian-
Tardenoisian stock when it is admitted to have brought
with it those very inventions which were the especial
marks of that stock ? The Azilian-Tardenoisians were the
world's earliest agriculturists, sailors and fishermen. So
were the Cabiri. The Cabirian cult seems to have originated
in the west. So did that of the Azilian-Tardenoisians, the
immigrants from Atlantis.

The Azilian-Tardenoisian people introduced the bow
and arrow into Europe. They were the bow-and-arrow
folk. The arrow, the dart, the lance is the special attribute
of the Cabiri. Like the Cabiri, too, they introduced the
art of writing, or rather the germs of that art. Their
" letters " were painted on pebbles, and bore a close resemblance to some of the Maya symbols of Central America,
which Americanists have named calculiform or " pebble-
shaped."

But I must not permit myself to be drawn by an interesting side issue from the main point, which this diversion is
after all intended to illustrate, that the worship of the

Cabiri can be traced to American soil, and that this alone is acceptable proof of its Atlantean origin.

We undoubtedly find a cult closely similar to that of the Cabiri in ancient Mexico. The gods Uitzilopochtli and Tezcatlipoca display in their worship, single and dual, all the signs familiar in that of the Cabiri.

In the first place we have the best evidence that these gods are brothers. "They (the Mexicans) say that the two are brothers," says Bernal Diaz (*Historia Verdadera*, Bk. VI, C. 91). Now let us glance at their insignia. Tez-

Mexican god Uitzilopochtli.

catlipoca invariably carries either the spear or the *atlatl*, the spear-thrower. He is the god of the spear *par excellence*. The Cabiri bear the insignia of Vulcan. Now Tezcatlipoca, like Vulcan, is lame. His myth, similar to that of Vulcan, tells us how he was cast out of heaven and became a cripple. Uitzilopochtli also carries the spear. Like the Cabiri or Dioscuri, each of these gods is connected with the stars, Tezcatlipoca presiding over the constellations of the North and Uitzilopochtli over those of the South. As the Cabiri were the gods of fire and wind so were Uitzilopochtli and Tezcatlipoca respectively, and the former was, like the Cabiri, associated with sundry pigmy figures which were placed round his idol in the great teocalli or temple of Mexico. Lastly, these Mexican gods were connected with the serpent, as were the twin Cabirian deities. They had also a mystic society of their own, the Warriors' House, in which strange rites were celebrated, and human sacrifice was offered to both.[1]

These numerous points of coincidence make it impossible that the resemblance between the cults could have been a fortuitous one. We find in both Europe and America a cult of which the deities are war-like twins armed with the lance, and connected with wind, fire, the stars and a definite mystical society. They are also associated with a myth strongly resembling that of Vulcan, and with pigmy images. That they are merely an American version of the Cabiri there can be no question. The Roman Castor and Pollux, the "heavenly twins," were merely a later Italian form of the Cabiri, and closely resemble the Mexican twin gods. In both cases these deities lead the warriors into battle and flourish the heavenly spear.

I believe that the cult of the Cabiri, European and American, emanated from Atlantis, that eastward it spread to North Africa and thence by Carthaginian agency to Greece and Asia Minor, and westward, by way of the Antilles, to Mexico and the American mainland in general.

If this be so, the worship of the aborigines of the Antilles will display signs of a similar cult. It does not fail to do so. We find that there existed in these islands *zemis*, or gods, known as Baidrama, or twins, also called Bugid y Aiba. Pane says that the natives believed that their strength could be augmented by these beings (which signifies that they were war-like), and that when they smoked in honour of them their arms increased in size. Professor Mason in his edition of Irving's *Columbus* (Vol. I, p. 333) states that a wooden image from the West Indies "represents two individuals seated on a canopied chair." Fewkes remarks that : "These figures were undoubtedly idols worshipped by the aborigines of the island upon which they were found. They probably stood in niches in caves or in special houses dedicated to them. The twinning of idols in one figure recalls statements of early authors that the great deity of the Haitians had two attendants to do her bidding. The author of this paper has referred to a twin amulet from Santo Domingo and has

[1] For a full description of these rites see my *Gods of Mexico*, pp. 66–116.

PLATE IV.—TWIN FORM OF ZEMIS.
Or idols from Antilles (after Fewkes).

heard of an image of clay composed of two united idols. All these figurines evidently represent the same or a very similar conception of Antillean mythology."[1]

These gods were associated with the serpent, as were the Cabiri. The priests of the West India Islanders, like the Pythoness of the Greeks and the Chilan of the Maya, were known as Boii, or serpents. Like the Cabiri and their Mexican analogues, too, the West Indian *zemis* were associated with the winds. They were also the centres of an elaborate secret ceremonial worship. This took the form of elaborate dances and dramatic representations, the same type of ceremony, in fact, as is found in the ancient Egyptian and Hellenic mysteries.

North of Mexico the Pueblo Indians of the South-western United States still preserve much of their prehistoric religious ceremony and culture. The Hopi in especial possess a most complicated system of priestly rite and tradition, most of which is associated with secret societies. One of these bodies, for example, specialises in snake-worship, another in ritual connected with the deer, and so forth. These rituals are predominantly religious and mystical, still they enshrine much practical knowledge regarding the care of seed, the proper season for planting and reaping. Anciently, it would seem, from the traditions of these people, they were in the habit of sacrificing newly born children to the serpent gods. We find almost the selfsame ritual occurring among the maize-growing tribes of the Central and Eastern United States. The Pawnees had a human sacrifice and an annual cycle of ceremonies centring in the cultivation of the maize plant. These mystical priesthoods naturally attracted to themselves every description of magical rite, as such bodies never fail to do, and some of them have developed into societies greatly at variance with their original form and intent.

There can be little doubt that a definite ritual connection exists between the secret and mystical societies of America and those of Europe and North Africa. The subject is a vast one, and it is impossible to do more than outline it here. There is, however, abundant evidence to prove that from Egypt to Mexico all such mysteries were

[1] *Aborigines of Porto Rico*, p. 201.

associated with one and the same complex, that all sprang from one and the same idea. That was the idea associated with the growth of grain. The several Egyptian mysteries, those strange secret societies of the ancient world, the rites of the Cabiri, of Eleusis, of Ceres, of Samothrace—all were connected with the growth of the grain. All growth is mysterious, and primitive man probably regarded it as in some manner magical. It is also noticeable that those mysteries, in the Old World at least, took place underground, in darkness, and that there was enacted the symbolism of the growth of grain, probably for the purpose of inciting the powers of growth to greater activity by dint of sympathetic magic.

In the first chapter of *The Book of the Dead*, the great compendium of Egyptian religious dogma, we encounter the phrase " I look upon the hidden things in Re-stau," an allusion to the ceremonies which were performed in the sanctuary of Seker, the god of death at Saqqara. These typified the birth and death of the sun-god, and were celebrated betwixt midnight and dawn. Again, in the one hundred and twenty-fifth chapter, we read, " I have entered into Re-stau, and I have seen the Hidden One who is therein." Herodotus, who is supposed to have been initiated into these mysteries, is rightly cryptic concerning them, and just as he has aroused our interest to fever-heat, he invariably sees fit to remark that his lips are sealed on the subject.

The mysteries connected with the worship of Osiris in Egypt arose out of the idea that the growth of the corn plant was a sacred and magical thing. In one of the chambers dedicated to Osiris in the great Temple of Isis at Philæ, the dead body of Osiris is represented with stalks of corn springing from it. The accompanying inscription tells us that " this is the form of him whom one may not name, Osiris of the mysteries, who springs from the returning waters." " It would be impossible," says Sir James Frazer, " to devise a more graphic way of depicting Osiris as a personification of the corn, while the inscription attached to the picture proves that this personification was the kernel of the mysteries of the god, the innermost secret that was only revealed to the initiated." We seem to observe references to a mystical society connected with the growth of corn in *The Book of the Dead*, which certainly dates from prehistoric times, and is most probably the developed ritual of a cult connected with the phenomena of growth. In its pages we find password and countersign, and all the magical material necessary to the ritual of such a secret cult as that we have been discussing.

In Greece the most important of the mysteries was perhaps the Eleusinian, and, indeed, we may take it as typical of the Hellenic mysteries as a whole. The chief figures in the cult of Eleusis were Demeter and Kore (or Persephone) and Pluto. All these are deities of the Underworld, and, like many other gods of that sphere, all the world over, they are also deities possessing an agricultural significance. Much remains uncertain regarding the actual ritual in the hall of the Mystæ, but one thing is certain, and that is that the ceremony was of the nature of a religious drama or passion-play, in which were enacted the adventures of Demeter and Kore, symbolic of the growth of the corn, the mother representing the old and the daughter the new plant. Hippolytus states that a cornstalk was shown to the worshippers at these mysteries. That in itself is sufficient to reveal their true character.

The mysteries of the Cabiriac worship were celebrated at Thebes and Lemnos, but especially in the isle of Samothrace. The time chosen was night. The candidate for initiation was crowned with a garland of olive, and wore a purple band round his loins. Thus attired, and prepared by secret ceremonies, perhaps mesmeric, he was seated on a throne brilliantly lighted, and the other initiates danced round him in slow and solemn measure.

As we have seen, we find mysteries of the same character in the New World. But in Asia, when found, and that scantily, they are obviously of late introduction. In America, however, they were of precisely the same nature as in ancient Greece and Egypt.

In the first place, the corn (in America, maize) ceremony is to be found in the West Indies. Gomara, writing of the principal ceremony of the Haitians, says : " They approached dancing, and singing to the sound of the shells. . . . They seated themselves like tailors, and prayed with a low voice. Then there approached many women bearing baskets of cakes on their heads and many roses, flowers and sacred herbs. They formed a circle as they prayed, and began to chant something like an old ballad in praise of the god. All rose to respond at the close of the ballad. They changed their tone and sang another song in praise of the cacique, after which they offered the bread to the idol, kneeling. The priests took the gift, blessed and divided it, and so the feast ended, but the recipients of the bread preserved it all the year, and held that house unfortunate and liable to many dangers which was without it."

It is in connection with the gods Uitzilopochtli and Tezcatlipoca, the Cabiri of Mexico, that the chief maize festivals of ancient Mexico were celebrated. At the feast of Tezcatlipoca, known as the Toxcatl, the priests made an image of his brother Uitzilopochtli in dough. This was placed on a litter decorated with wooden serpents and was divided among the people. The virgins who carried it wore wreaths of maize, and a great heap of maize flour was placed in the temple in which the footprints of the returning god were thought to be descried.

The occurrence of these grain mysteries in America thus affords further proof that the cult of the Cabiri, or some cult which had had a common origin with it, had been widely disseminated in the Western continent. We thus discover all the circumstances connected with a supposedly European cult in Mexico and elsewhere in America, and are forced to the conclusion that both emanated from a third and medial region.

But space is altogether lacking in which to draw further parallels between the mystical systems of the Old World and the New. There is, however, one circumstance relating to these which may briefly be touched upon. Plato, in his account of Atlantis, mentions that the Atlanteans indulged in bull sacrifice. The sacred bulls, he says, grazed near the Temple of Poseidon, and these the ten kings of the islands periodically offered up in sacrifice. From Egypt to the bison area of North America we find the cult of the bull flourishing. To be sure, several of the links are missing, and I do not desire to lay undue stress on such resemblances as exist. The bull was, perhaps, Europe's earliest symbol of godhead. On the walls of the caverns of Altamira and other caves in Northern Spain and in the Dordogne district of Southern France once inhabited by Crô-Magnon man, the bull is depicted with a liveliness and fidelity which the painters of Egypt and Assyria never approached. These caverns were, indeed, centres of a bull-worshipping cult. The Egyptian Serapeum or Temple of Apis is merely an architectural elaboration of the cave-shrines of the Dordogne. It was in early Spain and France, then, that the cult of the bull had its origin, spreading along the shores of the Mediterranean till it reached the Nile Valley, and carrying with it the rite of " taking the bull by the horns," or, as we should call it to-day, " the Rodeo." This rite was preparatory to the animal's sacrifice.

The practice spread to Crete. The art of Crete conclusively shows that " steer-wrestling " there was not only a recognised national sport but was attended by large crowds of fashionably attired spectators. So that there is really nothing new under the sun. The event took place in an area specially designed for the purpose. One of the most remarkable frescoes at Gnossos is that which portrays a crowd of Cretan notables looking on at a bout of bull-grappling. A fair, curly-headed Cretan youth is represented as gripping the bull by the horns and striving with all the might of his muscular arms to throw him, precisely as does the modern cowboy. To anyone who has seen a Rodeo, the resemblance is not to be mistaken. But the most convincing proof that the ancient Cretans celebrated the Rodeo with all the tireless zest of a Mediterranean people in such a sport is the great bull-ring which was discovered at Gnossos during its excavation. This resembles so much a modern Spanish bull-ring that no doubts can be entertained as to its former use for a similar purpose.

The Minotaur, the bull-headed god, is famous in legend as the deity of Crete. An annual tribute of maidens was delivered up to him for sacrifice in his labyrinthine retreat, which, like the Egyptian Serapeum, was evidently a reminiscence of the Pyrenean caves in which the bull was originally worshipped by Aurignacian man. That a very definite tradition of bull-wrestling and sacrifice obtained throughout the Mediterranean area cannot be gainsaid. From Crete it spread to Greece and Italy. It penetrated to ancient Palestine, where it was adopted by both Hebrew and Philistine. It has been advanced as a not impossible theory that those Philistines who were destroyed by Samson had gathered to amuse themselves with a display of bull-wrestling, and that, tired of their favourite sport, they had demanded that the blind champion of Israel be brought before them to exhibit his strength. Lastly it became the national sport of Spain, and still flourishes exceedingly in those parts of France formerly inhabited by Crô-Magnon man.

It is found in a weaker but none the less remarkable form among those Indians of the American plains whose livelihood was so closely associated with the bison. At certain festivals these dress as buffaloes, and go through an extraordinary and complex ritual reminiscent of Cretan, Egyptian and perhaps Aurignacian practice. But as I have said, the links are weak, and I do not care to press the analogy further, merely posing it as a remarkable but scarcely demonstrable evidence of what may have been an Atlantean rite in America.

These far-flung evidences may appear at first sight much too slender and scattered for serious recognition. Indeed they did to the writer until he discovered that *certain identical markings, doubtless magical, and described as " tectiform," or " roof-formed," by some anthropologists occur on the painted representations of buffaloes, both in the Aurignacian caves and in the drawings of the Plains Indians of America.* That these have no mere fortuitous resemblance will immediately be granted by any unbiassed person who chooses to give the designs a moment's comparative examination. They are practically identical, and must have originated in a common source. It will be observed that they occupy the selfsame position on the body of the animal. So far as I am aware, they do not occur in Asiatic art, late or primitive. To suggest that they are mere freaks of similarity is to expect too much of credence. They constitute merely one of the many resemblances between Red Indian and Aurignacian art.

We have seen, then, that American religion, in some of its phases at least, exhibits a connection with certain Old World forms the Atlantean origin of which is more than suspect, that a chain of associated customs with one missing oceanic link stretches from Egypt to America, and that Atlantean tradition appears to provide the missing connection; also that it is idle to look for traces of a European-American connection in Asia or Polynesia, as some modern authorities believe, not only because of the vast distances and natural obstacles which would have had to be traversed and overcome, but also because of the existence of complex social and religious conditions which would have swallowed up or altered out of all knowledge

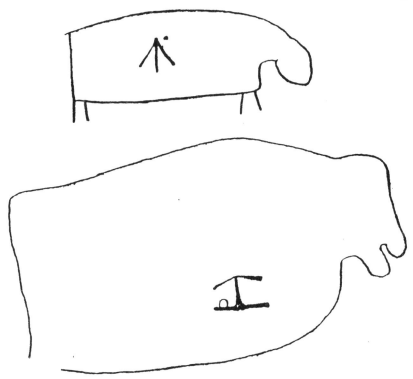

Outline sketches of (top) American Indian and (bottom) Aurignacian drawings of bisons, showing similar tectiform or tent-shaped devices.

such migrant cultural influences as essayed the long route from Spain to Central America by way of Asia. Surely it is much more scientific to suppose a single submerged stepping-stone in the Atlantic than to erect a hypothesis of tedious migration from Aurignacian Spain to North America; for not only do chronological conditions belie the possibility of such a pilgrimage, but the nature of the swarming cultural complexes to be traversed and penetrated render it well-nigh impossible that Aurignacian or Egyptian influences could have reached the American continent by the Asian route without undergoing a metamorphosis which would have rendered them unrecognisable on their arrival. The evidence shows that such Old World influences as reached America always did so in quite a recognisable shape, and frequently in their original form. That mummification or Crô-Magnon art reached America almost unaffected, and after countless centuries of pilgrimage, through the mesh and moil of Asiatic culture, is a theory, I think I will be able to prove, which is rendered none the less pathetically bankrupt because of its reiteration. Even if we suppose for the dissemination of Egyptian or European culture a race of missionary bearers, and designate them " The Children of the Sun," we must own that it is the most improbable thing in the world that a caste bearing even the entire knowledge of Egyptian civilisation could have penetrated the vast spaces of Asia or the Pacific to reach America at last, retaining the cultural complex it carried almost unaltered —which is, of course, not at all the same thing as saying that many Asiatic customs did actually find their way to America by devious routes and in altered forms.

CHAPTER VI

THE EVIDENCE FROM THE MUMMY

I WISH in this chapter to adopt the natural science method, to try to prove that the seeds of the art of mummification came from Atlantis and were broadcast to Europe and America, precisely as others have demonstrated the former existence of a land connection between the two continents through the resemblance of their flora and fauna. If this hypothesis be correct, we will find mummification, or the artificial preservation of the dead, occurring in its earlier forms in Spain and France, in the Canaries, the Antilles and the American mainland. As a matter of fact we do so most definitely, whereas those who seek to show that the custom spread from Egypt to America via Asia or Polynesia can point to no such continuous traces of it along these routes as it shows via the Atlantic route.

We certainly find the germs of these funerary practices which later developed into the elaborate rites of mummification in the burials of the Aurignacians in France and Spain. The bones, says Macalister, were frequently removed from the flesh, as is the case among certain American-Indian tribes. "The deposition," he says, "of offerings with the dead is quite sufficient to indicate a belief in a life after death, in which the dead will have need of the gifts placed in the tomb. Women, equally with men, shared in its privileges. The remarkable rite of painting the bones red should be especially noticed. . . . The purpose of the rite is perfectly clear. Red is the colour of living health. The dead man was to live again in his own body, of which the bones were the framework. To paint it with the colour of life was *the nearest thing to mummification that the Palæolithic people knew ; it was an attempt to make the body again serviceable for its owner's use.* In this connection it is instructive to recall a familiar incident in folk tales, in which the hero having come to grief, the flesh of his body is restored from the bones, or even from a small splinter of bone, and then resuscitated. . . . Already in 1877 Dr. Heinrich Wankel, speaking of the cave of Býčiskála in Moravia, where human remains were found along with bones of the cave bear, described it as ' the great cave where once the reindeer man lived, whose antechamber was the scene of a cult of the dead, where at a chieftain's grave human sacrifices were offered.' . . . It well expresses the feelings which these ancient caverns naturally excite, even in one who lives in the sceptical atmosphere of modern science. Later, Dr. Marett, in his essay on the cave of Niaux, quoted above, does not hesitate to call it a 'sanctuary,' and to treat it as such. The existence of fine paintings at the farthest ends of these great and complicated caverns ; the presence of the two splendid statuettes of bisons in the remotest recesses of Tuc d'Audoubert, are facts certainly suggestive of animal gods in their ' chambers of imagery.' "[1]

We may infer from this, then, that a cult of the dead obtained among the Aurignacian immigrants to Europe from Atlantis, that they practised " the nearest thing to mummification " they knew, that the conception of the preservation of a part of the body to render it serviceable for the owner's use was in vogue among the Crô-Magnons. This is the whole purpose and significance of mummification as found in Egypt and elsewhere. In early Egyptian essays at mummification the corpse is painted red as in the examples of the Aurignacian bones, and the Egyptians painted the statues of their gods red in order to endow them with life.

Nor do the Crô-Magnons of the Canary Islands, who, as we have seen, possessed the Aurignacian civilisation, disappoint us, for the art of mummification was found to be flourishing among them even at the period of their discovery by the Spaniards. Alonzo de Espinosa, a friar of the sixteenth century, tells us that the office of the embalmer in these islands was, as in Egypt, confined to a certain caste of men and women to whom the preservation of the dead of their respective sexes was entrusted. These people, as in the Nile country, were regarded as pariahs, and were abhorred by the rest of the population. After washing the corpse, they forced down the throat a mixture composed of melted mutton grease, " powder of heath " (grass seed ?), stones and the bark of pine trees, cramming down the preparation for the space of fifteen days, and placing the body in the sun, first on one side and then on the other, until it was dried. This process they called

---

[1] *Text-book of European Archæology*, pp. 502–3.

xaxo, or *jarco*, "the deceased," and the period during which it was carried out was one of mourning among the relatives, and was followed by no other rites or ceremonies. The corpse was then sewn up and enveloped in hides taken from certain sheep or goats selected and set apart for the purpose, and so marked that the mummy could afterwards be clearly recognised. These skins were tanned to the colour of chamois, and were sewn over with pine bark by means of thongs of the same material, and so skilfully that the seams were scarcely visible. Some of the more distinguished dead were placed in sarcophagi of a hard wood, carved in one piece, and in the shape of the body, precisely as were the Egyptian sarcophagi, and the corpse was then carried to some almost inaccessible cavern approached by a rude staircase cut in the face of the rock.

M. R. M. Gattefossé in his suggestive book *Adam : L'Homme Tertiare* (pp. 92–95) says that the dead among the Guanches were embalmed with care. The *xaxos*, or mummies, resembled those of Egypt in all particulars, except that the linen bands securing the latter were replaced by dressed skins. This treatment, he proceeds to say, has been found in many Neolithic tombs. The description which we possess of the Canarese method of embalmment appears so like that given by Herodotus of the Egyptian method as to be almost identical. The *xaxos* of the nobles were enclosed in sarcophagi of wood and placed in rows in artificial grottoes. In the Canaries, and without doubt anciently in Atlantis, he says, if the dead belonged to a family capable of bearing the expense, operations were commenced by laying the body on a great stone slab. An incision was then made in the stomach with a stone knife, and other operators removed the intestines, which were washed and cleansed. The body was also washed, especially the eyes, the interior of the mouth, the ears and the fingers, with water in which salt had been melted. Aromatic plants were then placed in the cavity of the trunk and the corpse was exposed to the sun. During this period of desiccation they treated the body with a kind of unguent made of grease and powdered aromatic plants, pine, resin and other absorbent essences, and it was also rubbed with antiseptic gums. On the fifteenth day the embalmment was regarded as complete and the corpse was returned to the relatives, sewn up in skins which had been prepared during the deceased's lifetime. It was then placed in the sarcophagus and disposed in the mortuary cave. Frequently this took the form of a tumulus or pyramid.

These Guanche mummies, many of which have been discovered in the Barranco de Fatago in Grand Canary, are usually found lying on the left side, wrapped in goatskin, with the hands crossed over the breast in the manner of some of the Peruvian mummies. They are, as a rule, placed in a crouching or sitting posture like that of the mummies of Mexico or Peru rather than stretched out in the Egyptian manner. Indeed the Guanche mummy in its general appearance and arrangement appears to resemble the American " mummy-bundle " much more than the elaborate examples of Egyptian funerary practice. Mexican mummies, as depicted in manuscripts and recovered from tombs, are usually sewn up in cotton sacks, and the more numerous embalmed bodies encountered in Peruvian graves and rock tombs are almost invariably found in a sitting posture.

In the view of Professor Elliot Smith " the technical procedures of embalming in West Africa and the Canary Islands were not adopted in Egypt until the XXIst Dynasty," or about 1000 B.C. We are thus left to draw the inference that they found their way from Egypt to the Canaries after 1000 B.C. But we have already seen that the germs of the art of embalming are to be observed *in Crô-Magnon practice* as Macalister states, and that, as Gattefossé remarks, the prototypes of Canarese mummies are to be found in Neolithic tombs which greatly antedate the XXIst Dynasty.

Mummification in Egypt was connected with ancestor worship, and was certainly developed out of the same ideas as that which prompted Crô-Magnon man to preserve the bones of his dead. The Osirian priesthood taught the sacredness of the human body, and believed that from it would re-arise the regenerated and purified spirit. The first forms of mummification in the Nile country, so far as it is possible to identify these as of early date, consist in merely drying the corpse in the sun, or treating it with a resinous preparation. As time progressed, this primitive treatment developed gradually into the elaborate rite and art of embalming, with its picturesque and long-drawn-out ceremonial. The graves of Beni Hassan show that by the time of the Middle Kingdom the internal organs had come to receive separate and special treatment, being placed in a box divided into four compartments inscribed with the sacred names of the four deities known as Canopic, who presided over them. But burials of this period are found in which the work has been " scamped," and it is apparent that the embalmers, instead of removing the intestines, made up parcels inscribed with their names, believing probably that a written statement that these bundles contained the heart, lungs and the rest was magically efficacious and quite as satisfactory as their presence in the receptacle prepared for them.

It is not until the period of the New Kingdom, that is, the XVIIIth to the XXVIth Dynasties, that the art of mummification reached any degree of elaboration. At first it was only the bodies of the Pharaohs, who were identified with Osiris, which received this elaborate treatment, but the need of a court in the Otherworld made it incumbent that the bodies of the nobility should also be preserved. Persons of wealth and rank took up the custom, and at last the corpses of even the poorest Egyptians were subjected to one or another process of embalming, of which pickling in a bath of natron was the most popular. By the time of the XXIst Dynasty the process had reached the height of its development, and a mummification of an elaborate kind cost about £700 in modern money. When the relations of the deceased consulted the professional embalmers they were shown models of mummies, one of which they selected. The corpse was then placed in the hands of the embalmers. First of all a corrosive was injected into the brain cavity, after which its almost liquid contents were removed through the nostrils. An embalmer, whose office rendered him a pariah, so sacred was the human body considered, made an incision in the corpse with a flint knife, an instrument connected with prehistoric practice. The intestines and principal organs were then removed, washed and steeped in palm wine. The body then underwent a drying process, and was stripped of its flesh, only the skin remaining, or was

stuffed with sawdust skilfully introduced through in-
cisions, so that the natural form was completely restored.
The cavity occupied by the organs might be packed with
myrrh, cassia or other spices. After being sewn up, the
corpse was pickled in a bath of natron for seventy days,
and then carefully bandaged with linen treated with some
adhesive substance. A coffin was built for it which retained the shape of the human form, and which was gaily
and elaborately painted with figures of divinities, amulets,
symbols and sometimes burial scenes.

The canopic jars in which the intestines were placed had
lids carved in the shape of human heads, but after the
XVIIIth Dynasty the heads of the four sons of Horus, the
Canopic deities so called, the man-headed Mesti, the jackal
Tuamutef, the ape-headed Hapi and the falcon Qebhsen-
nuf, the genii who guarded the north, east, south and west
respectively were represented upon their covers. In their
respective jars were placed the lungs and heart, the larger
intestines, the liver, the lesser intestines. These jars were
placed in the tomb beside the mummy.

The treatment of the mummy and the various ceremonies
in connection with its embalmment were undoubtedly
magical in origin. As each bandage was laid in its exact
position certain words of power were uttered which were
supposed to be efficacious in the preservation of the part
swathed. After consecration the priest uttered an invoca-
tion to the deceased and then took a vase of liquid containing ten perfumes, with which he smeared the body twice
from head to foot, taking especial care to anoint the head
thoroughly. The internal organs were at this juncture
placed on the body and the backbone immersed in holy
oil, supposed to be an emanation from the gods Shu and
Geb. Certain precious stones were then laid on the mummy,
each of which had its magical significance. Thus crystal
lightened his face, and carnelian strengthened his steps.
A priest who personified the jackal-headed god Anubis,
the sacred dog which led the deceased to the Otherworld,
then performed certain magical ceremonies on the head
of the mummy, and laid certain bandages on it. After a
further anointing with oil the deceased was declared to
have " received his head." His hand was then filled with
the thirty-six substances used in embalming, symbolical

PLATE V.—" CANOPIC " JARS.
From a grave at Zaachilla, Mexico.

of the thirty-six forms of the god Osiris, and he was rubbed with holy oil. Lastly, the toes were wrapped in linen, and after an appropriate address the ceremony came to a conclusion.

The point is that all this elaborate ceremonial had the significance not only of preserving the body but of rendering it as lifelike as possible. Thus while magic played its part in the maintenance of the corpse's fabric and everything possible was done to preserve it for ages, realism was observed in such details as the eyes, which were often made of ivory and obsidian, to seem as lifelike as possible, and even the body moisture was imitated in unguents and essences. Incense gave breath, and rouge or red paint the hues of life. *The whole was a mere elaboration of the Aurignacian practice of painting the bones red*, and that the flesh was removed from them, as among the Crô-Magnons, we have seen. *The Book of the Dead* and *The Book of the Opening of the Mouth*, which prescribe these rites, were so ancient that they well might have had their unwritten origins in Aurignacian times. A hieratic inscription upon the sarcophagus of Queen Khem-nefert, wife of Mentuhetep, a king of the XIth Dynasty (*ca.* 2500 B.C.), states that a certain chapter of *The Book of the Dead* was discovered in the reign of Hesep-ti, the fifth king of the Ist Dynasty, who flourished about 4266 B.C. That as early as 2500 B.C. a chapter of *The Book of the Dead* should be referred to a date almost 2000 years before that is astounding, and the mind reels before the idea of a tradition which, during comparatively unlettered centuries, could have preserved a religious formula almost unimpaired. Mark, too, that the chapter in question was " discovered " about 4266 B.C. If it was only discovered then, it must have been in existence for countless centuries before that in a spoken and traditional form, and indeed the epoch of its discovery is less than four thousand years in time from the latest dated Aurignacian remains, or two thousand years less than the lapse of time between the record of its discovery and the present day. In all probability it was brought eastwards with Aurignacian civilisation when that culture took an Oriental trend.

The embalmer's art, or its beginning, was disseminated throughout the Canaries and through Western Europe and

Africa until it finally reached Egypt. It has already been shown that the seeds of the art of mummification were spread broadcast from the Aurignacian area in France and Spain, that indeed the painting of the bones of the dead which obtained there was, as Macalister says, " the nearest thing to mummification " the Crô-Magnons knew. Doubtless the practice was quickened too by the adoption in that region in Neolithic times of binding the body with leather bands in order that its ghost should not walk. This practice seems to have spread to North Africa, and thence to Egypt, where it was greatly elaborated. Some such process of development too must have taken place in the West Indies and the American mainland. In all probability the Aurignacian corpses were, like those of the Guanches of the Canaries, wrapped up in skins, which could scarcely be expected to survive the many centuries between burial and the discovery of the interments. If we now cross the ocean to America, we find almost precisely similar rites obtaining. The Mexicans, Maya and Peruvians all embalmed the dead. But just as the earliest attempts at the preservation of the dead are naturally found in Aurignacian sites, so the last decadent vestiges of the practice are encountered in the Antilles or West India Islands. Writing on the mortuary customs of the aborigines of Porto Rico, Mr. J. H. Fewkes says : " The skull and other bones of the dead were wrapped in cotton cloth or basketry and preserved for worship. The crania were sometimes attached to bodies made of cotton in human form, and were kept in a certain house, generally that of the cacique. Human bones were treated as zemis (gods), and preserved for religious purposes. The Carib also made cotton images which contained human bones, which are thus referred to by Davies : ' They expect in their sickness the sentence of their life or death from those detestable oracles, which they receive by the means of these puppets of cotton, wherein they wrap up the worm-eaten bones of some wretched carcass, taken out of the grave. . . . They burn in honour of them the leaves of tobacco, and sometimes they paint their ugly shapes in the most considerable place of their vessels, which they call piraguas, or they wear hanging about their necks a little image representing some one of these cursed spirits.' Peter Martyr mentions seated Zemis made of cotton, but as objects of this kind are naturally perishable, few specimens have been preserved to the present time. One of these found in Santo Domingo, formerly owned by Señor Rodriguez, consisted of a skull inclosed in a cotton covering and mounted on a body stuffed with the same material. Apparently artificial eyes were inserted in the eye-sockets and cotton or other fabrics were tied about the legs and arms." Fewkes further states, quoting Oviedo, that at the burial of a Haitian cacique two wives were voluntarily buried alive with him. "Wife burial was not always practised, the customary method of interment being to bind the body with bandages of woven cloth and to place it in a grave along with the jewels and treasures most prized by the cacique in life." A crypt of sticks was built over the corpse in order that the earth should not touch it, and among the Haitians the dead were inhumed, mounds of earth being raised over the graves.

In an illuminating passage Mr. Fewkes says : " The Guarano, commonly called the Warraus, who live on the many islands of the delta of the Orinoco, according to Gumilla, place their dead in the water and allow fishes to strip the corpse of the flesh and soft parts. The skull and other bones are then preserved in a decorated basket which is hung from the roof of the house. Considering the relationship between the prehistoric peoples of the West Indies and the Orinoco tribes, this custom among the Guarano is highly significant. The mortuary customs of the Indians of the Orinoco vary greatly, and probably the same statement is applicable to the customs of the different West Indian Islands. . . . Throughout the West Indies, as among the tribes of the Orinoco, especial care seems to have been taken to preserve the skeletons of the deceased. There is evidence that the Carib of the Lesser Antilles sometimes place their dead in earthen jars, as recorded by im Thurn in speaking of a small island called Ballineux that was used as a cemetery. The Jamaicans placed their dead in caves or sometimes interred the bones, deposited in urns."[1]

According to Sir Hans Sloane, a native of Jamaica saw in the woods in the year 1677 " a cave in which lay human

[1] *Report of Bureau of Ethnology*, pp. 58, 71-2.

bones, all in order, also pots and urns wherein were bones of men and children." These pots were large and oval and of a dirty reddish colour. " On the upper part of the rim or ledge there stood out an ear, on which were made some lines." " The dead," writes Charlevoix, " were treated by the use of fire but were not interred until they were thought thoroughly emptied and dried by the fire."

The Orinoco Carib, according to Gumilla, exhume the dead at the beginning of the year, place the remains in a basket, and hang it from the roof of the house. The habit of preserving the skulls, bones and other parts of the body as objects of reverence seems to have been universal among the West Indians.

Las Casas says that the Indians of Haiti had certain statues made of wood which Columbus described in a letter to his sovereign, and adds that they placed in them the bones of relatives, giving the statues the names of the people to whom the bones belonged. A zemi or idol Faraguvaol was, like the mummied Osiris, found in the trunk of a tree and carried to a chief. He was able to escape from sacks, as the Egyptian ba or soul could escape from the mummy swathings.

Elsewhere Mr. Fewkes remarks : " The dead were sometimes wrapped in cotton cloth, and cotton puppets or effigies of stuffed cotton cloth in which the bones of the dead were wrapped are mentioned in early writings. One of the best of these is figured in an article by the author in his pamphlet on zemis from Santo Domingo. . . . The figure, which was found, according to Dr. Cronau, in a cave in the neighbourhood of Maniel, west of the capital, measures 75 centimeters in height. According to the same author the head of this specimen was a skull with artificial eyes and covered with woven cotton. About the upper arms and thighs are found woven fabrics, probably of cotton, following a custom to which attention has been already called. There is a representation of bands over the forehead." Here we see a distinct reminiscence of mummy bandaging, and a great gap in the abdomen of the figure conclusively shows that the intention of the maker was to represent an eviscerated corpse.

On the mainland of America there is abundance of evidence that the practice of embalming the dead obtained,

PLATE VI.—ZEMI FROM ANTILLES.

Showing reminiscence of mummy form in cotton wrappings and eviscerated abdomen.

especially in the more highly civilised centres, Mexico, Central America and Peru. In the two first-mentioned countries the custom of disposing of the dead by fire was associated with mummification, the body being first embalmed and then consumed on a funeral pyre. The method of preparing the mummy differed somewhat according to regional practice. In the Mexican Valley and the more southerly districts it was placed in a hunched-up position inside a much ornamented " mummy-bundle," the paintings and decorations on which took the place of those on the Egyptian coffin. This was covered by a network of rope, and on the top was placed a false head or mask, which connects these bundles with the zemis of the Antilles. In the province of Michoacan the body was disposed after embalmment in a recumbent attitude and swathed in many bandages, almost precisely as in Egypt.

We gain our knowledge of Mexican and Maya mummies principally from passing references in aboriginal and Spanish colonial manuscripts and histories, and from pictures in the native lienzas or paintings. In the case of the Maya of Central America, the bodies of chiefs and kings were buried in elaborate stone tombs and sarcophagi, accompanying which are canopic vessels closely resembling those of Egypt, and having lids representing, like them, the gods or Bacabs of the four parts of the compass.

The Egyptians associated certain colours with the several organs of the body and with the cardinal points. Thus red was associated with the north and the lungs, white with the south and the liver, yellow with the east and the stomach, and black with the west and the intestines. Among the Maya these colours and compass-directions were associated with the bodily organs in a strikingly similar manner, white being allotted to the north and the lungs, yellow to the south and the belly, red to the east and the larger intestines, and black to the west and lesser intestines. It will thus be seen that the colours and organs for the west agree precisely, and that the north agrees as to the organ associated with it. The organs in question were, as has been said, placed by the Maya in canopic jars bearing a close resemblance to those of Egypt. " Apparently," remarks Mr. D. A. Mackenzie in an essay on the subject in *Folklore* for June, 1923, " the Egyptian system of mummification which reached America was accompanied by the Egyptian doctrine in less modified form than one might be led to expect, especially when one considers how varied were the cultural influences to which these doctrines must have been subjected during the process of gradual transmission from Egypt and across the Pacific to America." But surely it is more credible that a resemblance so striking arose out of dissemination from a common centre now submerged in the Atlantic than that it slowly and painfully communicated itself by a devious Asiatic or Polynesian route from Egypt to America. I confess that to me it seems much more unscientific to believe that Egyptian theological ideas reached America practically unaltered after traversing the great welter of Asia than that both Egypt and America drew their beliefs from a common Atlantic source. The protagonists of this theory also hold that Buddhistic beliefs reached America via Asia. That they did so is very obvious. But there is a world of difference between the two theories. Buddhism, pure or alloyed, may well have penetrated America, indeed did so, at a period when it was practically a new faith, strong and living. But to infer that the dogmas of the Egypt of the XXIst Dynasty reached Central America in what was practically an unaltered etate after a lapse of eight hundred years, and by way of Asiatic or Polynesian regions teeming with opposing beliefs, is to ask too much even of credulity. The school which supports this thesis presupposes an ubiquitous caste of Egyptian origin which it describes as " The Children of the Sun." It might find a more fitting title for this nebulous and universal fraternity in " The Children of the Moon."

The Mexican Codex Magliabecchiano, preserved in the Biblioteca Nazionale in Florence, shows on sheet 60 the mummy-bundle of a Mexican warrior. The resemblance to the swathed upright figure of the dead Osiris in the Egyptian papyri is striking. Its symbolical insignia include a head-band or fillet bound in front with a clasp of turquoise mosaic, blue nose- and ear-plugs, and a fan or shoulder-band of paper. The head is decorated by an elaborate plume and the pennant of the war-god, its patron, and the hair is ornamented with balls of cotton, symbol of the deities of the Underworld, and reminiscent of the cotton make-up of the zemis of the Antilles. Accompanying it is the blue hairless dog which preceded it to the Mexican Hades, much as did the dog Anubis in the case of the dead Egyptian. It is also associated with a symbol which is similar to the *tat* sign interred with the Egyptian dead, and which was believed to provide them with a new backbone on resurrection.

In the same codex we find a somewhat similar painting —a mummy-bundle wrapped up in plain cotton cloth and secured by a net. The mummy itself wears the mantle dedicated to the departed, and the symbolism which accompanies it is practically the same as that observed in the former example. There also occurs in Mexico a symbolical form of the mummy-bundle which seems to have been a reminiscence of mummification. The clothing of the deceased was wrapped round a stick, a piece of jadeite was inclosed to represent a heart, along with a lock of the deceased's hair, which probably stood in lieu of the body itself. The whole evidently represents a late phase which aimed at dispensing with the long and troublesome process of embalming and at achieving a similar end—the preservation of the body of the dead—by magical means alone.

That certain Mexican gods were developed from the idea of the mummy is obvious enough from their pictured representations. For example, Tlauizcalpan-tecutli, the deity who represents the planet Venus, is pictured in the Codex Borbonicus and the Codex Borgia as a mummy, accompanied by the insignia of those warriors who died by sacrifice, and by the small blue dog, the companion of the dead. At the period of his festival a sham mummy-bundle was hoisted upon a pole, and around this the celebrants danced, as may be seen from the picture of the ceremony on page 28 of the Codex Borbonicus. In another picture in the Sahagun MS., now in the Biblioteca del Palacio at Madrid, priests are seen in the act of making the mock mummy, the head-mask, the paper ornaments and banners which accompanied it, and this seems to me to link up the process with the manufacture of cotton mummies in the Antilles, to which reference has been made.

In a manuscript entitled " Relacion de las ceremonios y

ritos de Michoacan " a good deal of information is supplied
with reference to the funerary customs of the people of
that Mexican province. It contains several pictures
relative to the process of mummification, in which we see
the deceased chieftain laid out for evisceration. A representation of the funeral procession shows the mummy
swathed in cotton bands on its way to the funeral pyre
which is to consume it, and surrounded by mourners, the
widow abasing herself precisely as did the women mourners
in Egypt, and blackening her brow and head with ashes.
Similar scenes are represented in wall-paintings in a tomb
at Chichen Itzá in Yucatan. Describing one of these,
Le Plongeon says : " Coh is now laid out, being prepared
for cremation. His body has been opened at the ribs to
extract the viscera and heart, which, after being charred,
are to be preserved in a stone urn with cinnabar, where the
writer found them in 1875."[1] Throughout Central America
many tombs have been discovered which in all their details
made it plain that a method of mummification similar to
that which obtained in ancient Egypt was in vogue in
these regions, but had been mingled with and somewhat
overlaid by native rites for the disposal of the body by
fire. On the cement floor of Tomb I, Mound 7, at Xoxo,
Oaxaca, Mexico, was found a remarkable set of funerary
urns, markedly resembling the canopic jars of Egypt.
These represent the four Bacabs or genii of the Maya
quarters of the compass, and contained the viscera of the
deceased.

In Peru the art of mummification was almost universal,
and was not associated with the disposal of the body by
fire. Mummies are to be encountered at apparently all
stages of the history of the native race. Megalithic tombs
and monuments contain them in the doubled-up posture
so common among early peoples all the world over. These
megalithic tombs, or *chulpas* as they are termed, are composed of a mass of rough stones and clay, faced with huge
blocks of trachyte or basalt, so put together as to form a
cyst, in which the mummy was placed. The door invariably faces the east, so that it may catch the gleams of the
rising sun—a proof of the prevalence of sun-worship.
Squier alludes to one more than 24 feet high. An opening

[1] Queen Môo and the Sphinx.

PLATE VII.—STATUETTE OF THE MEXICAN
GODDESS COATLICUE.

Represented as a mummy-bundle. In the Calle del Coliseo, Mexico.

PLATE VIII.—SCULPTURE REPRESENTING MAYA MUMMY.
From Stela P. Copan. The body is decorated with symbols
resembling those placed on Egyptian mummies.

18 inches square gave access to the sepulchral chamber, which was 11 feet square by 13 feet high.

Many of these *chulpas* are circular, and painted in gay primary colours. They are very numerous in Bolivia, an old Peruvian province, and in the basin of Lake Titicaca, a sacred region, they abound. The dead were wrapped in llama skins, on which the outline of the eyes and mouth were carefully marked. The corpse was then arrayed in other garments, and the door of the tomb walled up. In some parts of Peru the dead were mummified and placed in the dwelling-houses beside the living. In the rarefied air of the plateaus the bodies rapidly become innocuous.

On the Pacific coast the method of mummification was somewhat different. The body was reduced to a complete state of desiccation and was deposited in a tomb constructed of stone or adobe. Vases intended to hold maize or chicha liquor were placed beside the corpse, and copper hatchets, mirrors of polished stone, earrings and bracelets have been discovered in these burial-places. Some of the remains are wrapped in rich cloth, and vases of gold and silver were placed beside them. Golden plaques are often found in the mouths, symbolic of the sun. The bodies exhibit no traces of embalming, and are usually in a sitting posture. Some of them have evidently been dried before inhumation, whilst others are covered with a resinous substance. They are generally accompanied by the articles used in life ; the men have their weapons and ornaments, women their household implements, and children their toys. The dryness of the climate, as in Egypt, keeps these relics in a wonderful state of preservation. In the grave of a woman were found not only vases of every shape, but also some cloth she had commenced to weave, which her death had perhaps prevented her from completing. Her light brown hair was carefully combed and plaited, and the legs from the ankle to the knee were painted red, after the fashion in vogue among Peruvian beauties, while little bladders of toilet powder and gum were thoughtfully placed beside her for use in the life to come.

In the ancient Temple of the Sun at Cuzco, the capital of old Peru, the mummies of thirteen royal Incas were found by the invading Spaniards seated around the altar of the sun, and in the Temple of the Moon, hard by, the embalmed remains of their queens were discovered similarly disposed.

Skinner in his *State of Peru* affords us a glimpse of the methods of embalming still in vogue among the people of the Peruvian Andes in the early part of the nineteenth century. He says : " On the day of decease they put the body, with its insignia, into a large earthen vessel or painted jar, which they bury in one of the angles of the quarter, laying over it a covering of potter's clay, and throwing in earth until the grave is on a level with the surface of the ground. When the obsequies are over they forbear to pay a visit to it, and lose every recollection of the name of the warrior. The Roamaynas disinter their dead as soon as they think the fleshy parts have been consumed, and having washed the bones of the skeleton, they place it in a coffin of potter's clay, adorned with various symbols of death, like the hieroglyphics on the wrappers of the Egyptian mummies. In this state the skeleton is carried home, to the end that the survivors may bear the deceased in respectful memory, and not in imitation of those extra-ordinary voluptuaries of antiquity, who introduced into their most splendid festivals a spectacle of this nature, which, by reminding them of their dissolution, might stimulate them to taste, before it should overtake them, all the impure passions the human pleasures could afford them. A space of about a year being elapsed, the bones are once more inhumed, and the individual to whom they belonged forgotten for ever."

Later I will adduce evidence to show that, like the pyramids of Egypt, those of Mexico and Peru were the last resting-places of kings and priests. That some American mummies at least were the objects of ritual for generations subsequent to their embalmment is proved by the state-ment of Mr. W. H. Holmes, who says that : " An extra-ordinary example of objective mnemonic record is furnished by the practice of the Incas of Peru. The mummied bodies of the earlier rulers were brought at stated periods and awarded the same daily service by their descendants as when living. By this practice a body of memories relating to the most important personages and events relating to the history of the nation, extending over a period of several hundred years, was preserved ; yet the record thus kept alive was necessarily restricted in scope and in a few generations must have become in large part vague and merged with myth."

Plenty of evidence is forthcoming to show that the art of mummification existed in other parts of North and South America in a more or less debased form. The Indians of Kentucky dried the body and filled it with sand, wrapping it in skins or matting, and placing it in a hut or cavern. In the Darien region the dead were eviscerated and the body was filled with resin, after which the corpse was smoked for preservation and kept in the ancestral hut. The Indians of Virginia removed the skin, and at a later stage restored it to the skeleton. In the island of Marajo in the Amazon delta large buried vases are discovered resembling the sarcophagi of Egypt in their symbolic ornamentation. Says Holmes : " Many of the Marajo vases are of large size and are tastefully embellished with human and animal features in relief, the relief motifs being elaborated in complicated and often formal designs in colour. Other vases of varied shape and size are embellished with incised and carved geometrical patterns, often labyrinthine, showing excellent taste. These embellishments are distinct from those of the more southern regions as well as those of the western highlands, but appear to resemble the decorative art of the Guianas and the West Indies. A number of very striking and handsome vessels obtained from graves and caverns in the valley of the Couanani are manifestly the work of related peoples."

According to Pinkerton, the Indians of Maryland and Virginia preserved their dead as follows : " Their bodies are first bowelled, then dried upon hurdles till they be very dry, and so about the most of their joints and neck they hang bracelets and chains of copper, pearl and such-like as they used to wear. Their inwards they stuff with copper beads, hatchets and such trash. Then lap they them very carefully in white skins, and so roll them in mats for their winding-sheets. And in the tomb, which is an arch made of mats, they lay them orderly."[1]

The Congaree or Santee Indians of South Carolina, according to Lawson, used a process of partial embalmment. Schoolcraft, in his *History of the Indian Tribes,*

[1] *Collection of Voyages*, Vol. XIII, p. 39.

quotes him as follows : " As soon as the party is dead
they lay the corpse upon a piece of bark in the sun,
seasoning or embalming it with a small root beaten to
powder, which looks as red as vermilion. The same is
mixed with bear's oil to beautify the hair. After the
carcass has laid a day or two in the sun they remove it
and lay it upon crotches cut in purpose for the support
thereof from the earth. Then they anoint it all over with
the aforementioned ingredients of the powder of this root
and bear's oil. When it is so done, they cover it over very
exactly with the bark of the pine or cypress tree to prevent
any rain to fall upon it. . . . As soon as the flesh grows
mellow and will cleave from the bone they get it off and
burn it, making the bones very clean, then anoint them with
the ingredients aforesaid, wrapping up the skull very carefully in a cloth artificially woven in opposum's hair. The
bones they preserve in a wooden box, every year oiling and
cleansing them. . . . The Indians make a roof of light
wood or pitch-pine over the graves of the more distinguished, covering it with bark and then with earth, leaving
the body thus in a subterranean vault until the flesh quits
the bones. The bones are then taken up, cleaned, jointed,
clad in white-dressed deer skins, and laid away in the
Quiogozon, which is the royal tomb or burial-place of their
kings and war-captains, being a more magnificent cabin
reared at the public expense. This Quiogozon is an object
of veneration, in which the writer says he has known the
king, old men and conjurors to spend several days with
their idols and dead kings, and into which he could never
gain admittance."

W. H. Dall, writing of the mortuary customs of the
Indians of the North-west coast, says : " The bodies were
eviscerated, cleansed from fatty matters in running water,
dried, and usually placed in suitable cases in wrappings of
fur and fine grass matting. The body was usually doubled
up in the smallest compass, and the mummy-case, especially in the case of children, was usually suspended (so as
not to touch the ground) in some convenient rock shelter.
Sometimes, however, the prepared body was placed in a
life-like position, dressed and armed. . . . The hunter was
dressed in his wooden armour, and provided with an enor-
mous mask, all ornamented with feathers, and a countless

variety of wooden pendants, coloured in gay patterns.
. . . Amongst the articles represented were drums, rattles,
dishes, weapons, effigies of men, birds, fish and animals,
wooden armour of rods, scales of wood and remarkable
masks, so arranged that the wearer when erect could only
see the ground at his feet." A treasure almost as various
as that found in the mausoleum of Tutankhamen !

Sauer, who accompanied Billings's expedition in 1802,
mentions that the Aleutian Islanders embalmed their dead,
and an article in the *San Francisco Bulletin* speaks of the
discovery of a cave full of Aleutian mummies by a certain
Captain Hemming.

That preservation of the bones was practised in lieu of
mummification by many American tribes who had not the
means for embalmment at their disposal is made clear by
Brinton, who remarks : " They thought *the soul would
return to the bones*, that these would clothe themselves with
flesh, and that the man would rejoin his tribe. *That this
was the real, though often doubtless the dimly understood
reason of the custom of preserving the bones of the deceased,
can be shown by various arguments.*[1] This practice was
almost universal. East of the Mississippi nearly every
nation was accustomed at stated periods—usually once in
eight or ten years—to collect and clean the osseous remains
of those of its number who had died in the intervening
time, and inter them in one common sepulchre, lined with
choice furs, and marked with a mound of wood, stone and
earth. Such is the origin of those immense tumuli filled
with the mortal remains of nations and generations which
the antiquary, with irreverent curiosity, has so frequently
chanced upon in all portions of our territory."

He proceeds to say that " A widow among the Takhalis
was obliged to carry the bones of her deceased husband
wherever she went for four years, preserving them in a
casket handsomely decorated with feathers." " So great
was the filial respect for these remains by the Indians that
on the Mississippi, in Peru and elsewhere, no tyranny, no
cruelty, so embittered the indigenes against the white
explorers as the sacrilegious search for treasures perpe-
trated among the sepulchres of past generations."

Farther on he remarks : " In some of the gentes in

[1] Italics are mine.

various parts of the continent there prevailed a belief that
the soul would somehow return to the eponymous ancestor. . . . The question has been debated and variously
answered whether the art of mummification was known
and practised in America.   Without entering into the
discussion, it is certain that the preservation of the corpse
by a long and thorough process of exsiccation over a slow
fire was nothing unusual, not only in Peru, Popoyan, the
Carib countries and Nicaragua, but among many of the
tribes north of the Gulf of Mexico. . . . *The object was
essentially the same as when the bones were preserved*, and in
the case of rulers the same homage was often paid to their
corpses as had been the just due of their living bodies.
The opinion underlying all these customs was that a part
of the soul, or one of the souls, *dwelt in the bones*, that these
were the seeds which, planted in the earth, or preserved
unbroken in safe places, would, in time, put on once again
a garb of flesh and germinate into living human beings."[1]

That the bones so preserved were frequently painted
red, as in the case of Crô-Magnon remains, proof is also
forthcoming.   Holmes states that in ancient burials in
Maine " the occurrence of red oxides . . . has led to the
use of the designation ' the red paint people.' "

It would seem then that, just as it has been possible to
demonstrate the former existence of a land connection
between Europe and America through the presence of
similar plants and animals in both of these now separated
areas, it is also possible to prove it by the persistence of
similar vestiges of ancient culture in both continents.   The
custom of mummification can be traced in the Canary
Islands and the Antilles.   On the west it penetrated the
interior through Central America to Mexico and the North,
and on the south-west to Bolivia and Peru, and vestiges
of it are to be found in Brazil.   On the east it spreads from
the Canaries and North Africa to Egypt, and its earliest
manifestation, the preservation of the bones of the dead,
is apparent in the Aurignacian regions of Spain and France.
Thus it is perfectly reasonable to infer that the two great
areas where it most generally flourished, *and whose insular
outposts are rich in its manifestations*, must have drawn
their   original   knowledge   of   mummification   from   one

[1] *Myths of the New World*, pp. 298 ff.

common centre. Where we find two broken pieces of a chain with isolated links lying in between, it is surely not unreasonable to suppose that all once belonged to one unbroken chain. One or two of the links, perhaps, are lost, but no sane man will doubt that they once actually existed.

Nor will it serve to advance the theory that the cult of mummification may have originated independently in the Old World and in the New. There is no cultural analogy for crediting the manifold origin of any custom so definite in its ritual and so well-marked in its minor details. The art of embalming arose out of the belief that the bones, and at a later date the body, must be rendered immortal in order to subserve the purposes of an immortal soul. This is not among those beliefs which can be classed as " natural " or primitive, but presupposes a cult not only of distinctly local and tribal but of very gradual development. A thousand circumstances, logical as well as fortuitous, must have gone to the making of what was a highly developed art as well as a religious creed rich in observances of quite extraordinary minuteness, and specialised as perhaps no other cult ever has been, and when we observe the minutiæ of the rites of mummification approaching each other so closely as they do in the Old World and the New, there appears to be little else to do than accept them as having arisen from a common source. The Old and New World systems arose on slightly different lines out of the Aurignacian, that is Atlantean, practice of preserving and painting the bones of the dead in the hope that these would once again be clothed in flesh and provide a house for the spirit. Such a custom was bound to develop into the more elaborate system of mummification. Indeed we have seen that it actually did so in Neolithic times. The preservation and painting of the bones was not only the germ-custom of mummification. It contained the *spirit* of its development as well, as all embryos do. It was this custom, this germ, which sprang from Atlantis, and which developed in the eastern and western continents on slightly different but inevitable lines.

Equally fatuous is it to try to demonstrate the introduction of mummification into America from Asia. It would be absurd, of course, to say that no customs connected with the art or ritual of embalming reached America from Egypt by way of Asia. But the evidence that the main current of the art reached America from Asia is much more slender than that which proves its Atlantean provenance. The links provided by Asiatic embalming are few and widely scattered, and have all the signs of late origin. Nor are the resemblances they display to African and American examples nearly so precise as the likenesses between these systems. Had mummification been conveyed from Asia to America it would have left traces much more definite and profound in the Far East than it has done. The same reasons preclude the possibility of its having reached America by way of Polynesia.

If it be maintained that the art of mummification originated in Egypt, in what manner, it may be asked, did it find its way thence to the Canary Islands ? It may be said that Phœnician voyagers found their way to the Canaries at an early date, and that they conveyed there men of Egyptian race. But even if they had done so, it is highly improbable that these were of the pariah caste who alone possessed the secret of the process of embalming, or of the priestly caste who had the necessary ritual knowledge to instruct the natives in the ceremonies of embalming as carried out in the period of the XXIst Dynasty. The contention for a direct Egyptian introduction is absurd, and if it be argued that the practice in Egypt and the Canaries arose from a common source in North Africa, that source has yet to be discovered. It seems much more logical to infer that it was oceanic, especially as the entire process is reflected on the other side of the Atlantic, and has well-defined links in its islands, both European and American.

We may conclude then that :

(1) The burial customs of the Crô-Magnons of Spain and France provide the first signs of the growth of the art of preserving the dead.

(2) That the art of mummification was practised in the Canary Islands, where the Crô-Magnons of Atlantis were marooned.

(3) That the remains of the process are discovered in the West India Islands.

(4) That it was practised elaborately, and much in the

same manner as in Egypt and the Canary Islands, in Mexico and Peru.

(5) That it could not have reached America by way of Asia in early times, all evidence that it did so being lacking.

(6) That only one link in the progression of the practice of embalmment is missing between Europe and America and the insular archipelagoes thereof, and that this link must formerly have been supplied by Atlantis.

CHAPTER VII

THE EVIDENCE FROM WITCHCRAFT

ANOTHER manifestation of Aurignacian culture found both in Europe and America more saliently than elsewhere is the strange cult known as witchcraft, with its host of rites and subsidiary superstitions. It is indeed quite a simple matter to prove that witchcraft, as discovered in America, is much nearer in its relationship to the witchcraft of Western Europe than to any similar system in Asia. Also it is demonstrable that in Asia the cult has taken a form strongly dissimilar from that in which it is found in Europe.

Witchcraft may be generally, if not particularly, described as a female magical cult, probably originating in a very early worship of the bull or the goat as a symbol of fertility by women who hoped for offspring. In the course of ages there grew up around it accretions of feminine lore, magical and medicinal, which survived well into modern times. But the point of most immediate importance in this place is that it was found in its most salient aspects in precisely those regions which must have been affected by immigration from Atlantis—in France, Spain and Mexico —and in the Aurignacian area of the two former countries. In fact its range is much the same as that of the early customs which later developed into mummification.

We must sharply discriminate between witchcraft and mere sorcery or shamanism. The former displays very special attributes and tendencies which the latter systems do not possess. For example, it is almost exclusively female, it is corybantic, or connected with the dance, it is associational, not individual, as are sorcery and shamanism, the ministers of which work alone. Let us see, then, what evidence we have of its existence in Aurignacian times, and what proof we have that the witchcraft of America is one and the same as that of Europe.

In a rock-shelter on a hillside at the village of Cogul, near Lerida, in Spain, several remarkable paintings have been discovered which were executed by Aurignacian or Crô-Magnon man. One of these depicts a number of women wearing skirts and peaked hats, precisely like those of the witches of later times, dancing round a male idol or priest who is painted black. The whole scene might well refer

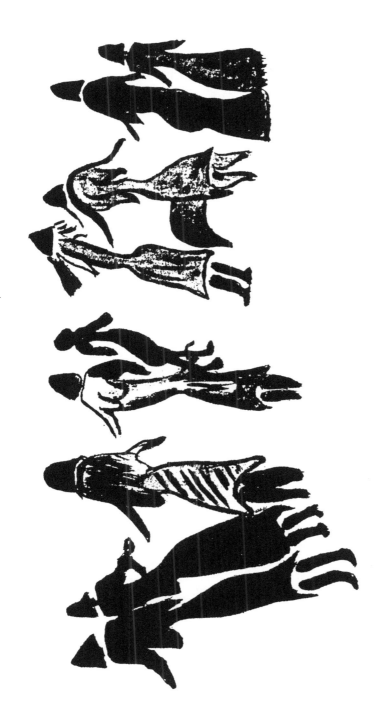

PLATE IX.—DANCE OF WITCHES ROUND IDOL.
Aurignacian art from Cogul.

to a sabbatic dance of witches in the fifteenth or sixteenth century. It shows conclusively that the cult of witchcraft was practised among the Aurignacians at an age immensely remote—ten thousand years ago, at the least computation.

The witch-cult in Mexico circulated round the idea of the Ciuateteô or Ciuapipiltin. Of these Sahagun says: " The Ciuapipiltin, the noble women, were those who had died in childbed. They were supposed to wander through the air, descending when they wished to the earth to afflict children with paralysis and other maladies. They haunted cross-roads to practise their maleficent deeds, and they had temples built at these places, where bread offerings in the shape of butterflies were made to them, also the thunder-stones which fall from the sky. Their faces were white, and their arms, hands and legs were coloured with a white powder. Their ears were gilded and their hair done in the manner of the great ladies. Their clothes were striped with black, their skirts barred in different colours, and their sandals were white." He further mentions that when a woman who had died in her first childbed was buried in the temple-court of the Ciuateteô her husband and his friends watched the body all night in case young soldiers or magicians should seek to obtain the hair or fingers as protective talismans.

Numerous chroniclers testify that the witches' sabbath was quite as notorious an institution in ancient Mexico as in mediæval Europe. But in the days prior to the coming of the Spaniards it was thought of as being celebrated by the dead rather than by the living. The Ciuateteô, or haunting mothers, out of envy for their more fortunate sisters and their offspring, continued to haunt the world at certain fixed periods, wreaking their spite upon all who were so unlucky as to cross their path. They are represented in the ancient Aztec paintings as dressed in the garments and insignia of the goddess Tlazolteotl, the witch *par excellence*, with a fillet and ear-plug of unspun cotton, a golden crescent-shaped nasal ornament, empty eye-sockets, and the heron-feather headdress of the warrior caste, for the woman who died in childbed was regarded as equally heroic with the man who perished in battle. The upper parts of their bodies were nude, and round the hips they wore a skirt on which cross-bones were painted.

They carried the witch's broom of *malinalli* grass, a symbol of death, and they are sometimes associated with the serpent, the screech-owl, and other animals and birds of ill-omen. These furies were supposed to dwell in the region of the west, and as some compensation for their early detachment from the earth-life, were permitted to accompany the sun in his course from noon to sunset, just

One of the Ciuatoteô, or Mexican witches, from the Codex Borgia.

She is about to sacrifice a child, and stands before an urn filled with human hearts. She wears the cotton spindle of the earth goddess, her skirt is decorated with lunar emblems and she is adorned by the lunar nose plate.

as the dead warriors did from sunrise to noon. At night they quitted their occidental abode, the Ciutlampa, or " Place of Women," and revisited the glimpses of the moon in search of the feminine gear they had left behind them—the spindles, work-baskets and other articles used by Mexican women. The Ciuatcteô were especially potent for evil in the third quarter of the astrological year, and

those who were so luckless as to meet them during that
season became crippled or epileptic. The fingers and
hands of women who had died in bringing forth were
believed by magicians, soldiers and thieves to have the
property of crippling or paralysing their enemies or those
who sought to hinder their nefarious calling, precisely as
Irish burglars formerly believed that the hand of a corpse
grasping a candle, which they called " the hand of glory,"
could ensure sound sleep in the inmates of any house they
might enter.

Sahagun says : " It was said that they vented their
wrath on people and bewitched them. When anyone is
possessed by the demons with a wry mouth and disturbed
eyes, with clenched hands and inturned feet, wringing his
hands and foaming at the mouth, they say that he has
linked himself to a demon. The Ciuateteô, housed by the
crossways, have taken his form." From this and other
passages we may be justified in thinking that these dead
women were also regarded as succubi, haunters of men,
lamias, compelling them to dreadful amours, and that they
were credited with the evil eye is evident from the statement that their glances caused helpless terror and brought
convulsions upon children, and that their jealousy of the
handsome was proverbial. We see, too, that like the
witches of Europe, they were associated with the " thunder-
stone," or elf-bolt, the prehistoric flint arrow which was
supposed to fall from the sky.

The divine patroness of these witches—for witches they
are called by the old friar who interprets the Aztec Codex
Telleriano-Remensis—who flew through the air on their
broomsticks and met at cross-roads, was Tlazolteotl, a
divinity who, like all deities of growth, possessed a plutonic
significance. The broom is her especial symbol, and in the
native Aztec MS. known as the Codex Fejèrvàry-Mayer
(sheet 17) we have a picture of her which represents her
as the traditional witch, naked, wearing a peaked hat, and
mounted upon a broomstick. In other places she is seen
standing beside a house accompanied by an owl, the whole
representing the witch's dwelling, with medicinal herbs
drying beneath the eaves. Thus the evidence that the
haunting mothers and their patroness present an exact
parallel with the witches of Europe seems complete. The

cult of the Mexican Nagualists of post-Columbian times was also permeated with practices similar to those of European witchcraft, and we read of its adherents smearing themselves with ointment to induce levitation, flying through the air, and engaging in wild and lascivious dances, precisely as did the adherents of Vaulderie or the worshippers of the Italian witch-mother Aradia, or, indeed, as the witches of our own island.

It is also clear that living women of evil reputation desired to associate themselves with the Ciualeteô. Says the interpreter of the Codex Vaticanus A.: "The first of the fourteen day-signs, the house, they considered unfortunate, because they said that demons came through the air on that sign in the figures of women, *such as we designate witches*, who usually went to the highways, where they met in the form of a cross, and to solitary places, and that when any bad woman wished to absolve herself of her sins she went alone by night to these places and took off her garments and sacrificed there with her tongue (that is drew blood from her tongue) and left the clothes which she had carried and returned naked as the sign of the confession of her sins."

Acosta says: "Some of these sorcerers take any shape they choose, and fly through the air with wonderful rapidity and for long distances. They will tell what is taking place in remote localities long before the news could possibly arrive. . . . To practise this art the sorcerers, usually old women, shut themselves in a house, and intoxicate themselves to the degree of losing their reason. The next day they are ready to reply to questions."

But we have further evidence from Mexico that an entire college of witches existed in the Huaxtec region near the coast, and that it was at one time sufficiently powerful to invade the Valley of Mexico in Toltec times. These witches appear to have succeeded in establishing superiority at Tollan, the capital, and in order to celebrate their victory, resolved to sacrifice a large number of prisoners to their patron goddess. Addressing their captives, they said: "We desire to drench the earth with you, to hold a feast with you, for till now no battle-offerings have been held with men." The Huaxtec country, whence they came, was a rich and closely settled agricultural area, its people were of Maya or Central American stock, and its chief goddess, Tlazoltcotl, whose priestesses these women were, represented the earth-mother, the bounteous giver of all fruits and grain. But they believed that this Mexican Ceres, worn-out by the production of foodstuffs, required occasional refreshment. This had formerly been administered by pouring libations of the blood of animals on the hard, cracked tropical soil, which appeared to absorb them thirstily. But, flushed with triumph, these Amazons resolved to offer up a sacrifice which should outvie all former oblations. It is also clear from their menacing speech that the festival was intended to take the form of a cannibal feast, a thing until then unheard of in Mexico, as their own statement seems to make plain. The native records insist upon the fact that the institution of ceremonial cannibalism was due to these witches, for such there is abundant evidence they were. Like the Hexen, or witches of ancient Germany, they seem to have had a penchant for human flesh, and further resembled that cult in their tendency to vampirism.

That mummification and witchcraft originally belonged to one and the same culture-complex seems fairly clear from the curious circumstance that the witches of Europe prized above all things a piece of Egyptian mummy-flesh as a vehicle for their magical operations. Throughout the witch-literature of Europe the mummy is constantly alluded to as part of the magical apparatus of the witch. When she failed to obtain it she had recourse to using earth taken from a newly made grave as a substitute. So far as I am aware, we do not find this practice in Eastern Asia, but that it was in vogue in America is substantiated by more than one instance. Allusion has already been made to the magical employment of the hands and fingers of dead women in Mexico, and Dawson, in his *Rites and Observations on the Kwakiool People of Vancouver*, alludes to an interesting case of it in that part of America. He says that when a Kwakiutl wizard desired to bewitch anyone, he tried to procure a lock of his hair, or a part of his clothing. "These are placed with a small piece of the skin and flesh of a dead man, dried and roasted before the fire, and rubbed and pounded together. The mixture is then tied up in a piece of skin or cloth, which is covered over with spruce gum. The little package is next placed in a human bone, which is broken for the purpose and afterwards carefully tied together and put within a human skull. This again is placed in a box, which is tied up and gummed over and then buried in the ground in such a way as to be barely covered. . . . This is done at night or the early morning and in secret, and is frequently repeated until the enemy dies." The drying of the human remains over a fire shows quite clearly that what was desired was a piece of flesh capable of desiccation and admixture with other elements, as in the operations of European witches. Benzoni tells us that the medicine men among the Borenqueños of the West Indies took some small bones and a little flesh and powdered them together as a purgative for the sick.

I think I have adduced sufficient and novel evidence to prove that the relationship between European and American witchcraft was much more intimate than that between either of these systems and any other sorcery cult. Most of the sorcery cults of the Far East are male organizations, whereas the essentially feminine character of witchcraft, both in its European and American manifestations, is clear. It is also obvious that it was known among the Crô-Magnons, the first immigrants from Atlantis to Europe, and this, indeed, is the very earliest proof we have of its existence anywhere. These similarities, when taken into consideration along with the geographical occurrence of the cult, seem to me much too powerful to be ignored, especially when we remember that the ancient Aurignacian area was, in later times, the very headquarters of Vaulderie or witchcraft in Europe. We find in ancient Mexico, as in Europe, a feminine cult connected with the worship of a fertility deity, whose ministers fly through the air on broomsticks, and, like the witches of Europe, smear themselves with ointments to assist levitation. Their queen, or tutelary deity, is depicted as nude, and bestriding a broom, and as wearing the traditional hat of bark. They are associated with the owl, and have skill in the herbalist's art. They induce falling sickness, as did the witches of France and Britain. They meet at cross-roads, where they celebrate their dreadful orgies, dancing to the flute of Tezcatlipoca, the demon-god, who bears a strong resem-

blance to the "big black man," the satanic figure of
Scottish witch-tradition, and who is obviously one and the
same as the sable figure portrayed in the Cogul Aurignacian
dance.

I might draw many other parallels between the witch-
cults of Europe and America, but these are the broad
essentials, and must suffice for the illustration of my
theory. But did witchcraft, or any similar feminine cult,
flourish in Atlantis itself? Persistent notices of it recur
in Greek mythological tales of the Gardens of the Hes-

Tlazolteotl, Queen of the Mexican witches, riding on a broomstick.

perides, situated in the Fortunate Isles of the Atlantic
area which, if they refer to any locality there, must surely
have done so to Atlantis. We also find a well-marked
female cult flourishing among the Guanches of the Canary
Islands, the last remnants of Atlantis.

Perusing the traditions which refer to the Hesperides or
Fortunate Islands, which are identified by many writers
with Atlantis, we find them associated with two distinct
female cults, the war-like Amazons and those strange
sorceresses, the Gorgons. The Amazons, says Diodorus
Siculus, dwelt on the island Hesperia, between Mount
Atlas in Africa and the ocean, and invaded the territory

of the inland mountaineers and their coastal neighbours, the Gorgons, whom they subjugated, until the latter rose to power again under their great queen Medusa, who was finally slain and conquered by Perseus. Says Mr. W. H. Babcock : " Both the Gorgons and the Western Amazons seem to have had their abodes on the shores of the Atlantic Ocean south of the Strait of Gibraltar, along the front of what we now call Morocco and the region south of it. We cannot say how much of these tales belong to Diodorus ; but he certainly did not invent the whole of them, and is not likely to have contrived their most distinctive features. The myth of Perseus, like that of Theseus and the Minotaur, meant something dimly and distantly historic. We think we partly understand the latter after the excavations in Crete. Similarly the flights and feats of Perseus, as given in mythology, may be another way of saying that he made swift voyages far afield, and descended on his enemies with deadly execution."[1]

The Amazonian armies were composed entirely of virgins, who married when their military service was completed. This is no improbable circumstance, for the same practice obtained in early Spain and North Africa in Hannibal's time, also in Dahomey before the break-up of that kingdom, with its cannibalistic rites, in the last century. Under their chieftainess Mirina, they attacked the region of Atlas in Africa with 30,000 infantry and 2000 cavalry. It was precisely from this region that Hannibal in later times drew the bulk of his Amazonian cavalry-women. Their shields were made of serpent skin, their offensive weapons were the lance and the bow. They passed into the territory of the Gorgons, on whom they inflicted immense slaughter, and pursued their conquering careers into Egypt and Syria.

" Am Azon," remarks that most interesting of all French writers on Atlantis, M. R. M. Gattefossé, of Lyons, " is in modern Berber Al Azoun, and signifies ' the people of Azoun ' in Algiers." He proceeds to draw the conclusion that this Azoun was the mother-goddess worshipped after the disappearance of Atlantis, in Ireland and among the Celts, under the name of Ana or Danu, who, he thinks, was one and the same with Neith, Athena and Urania. All

[1] *Legendary Islands*, pp. 16–17.

these goddesses had certainly attributes in common. The nations abutting on the region of the sunken Atlantis were, he states, addicted to the feminine cult rather than the male. In the rites of the people of Ouargia, the most ancient city of the desert, inhabited by the descendants of the Amazons, a dance was performed in which the young women of the town imitated the undulations of the serpent, and this he compares with the similar dances of the Nahuatls and Huichols of Mexico.[1]

Now, as we have seen, a similar Amazonian tribe flourished in Mexico, the sorceresses who invaded the interior from the coast, who were known as Ixcuiname, " the Four-Faced," the worshippers of Tlazolteotl. Their chief weapon, like that of the Amazons, was the bow, and they sacrificed their war captives to the goddess by shooting them with arrows. These women were assuredly witches as well as Amazons or warrior-women, for their patroness was Tlazolteotl, the chief of the dead witch-women, the Ciuateteô, alluded to above, and was also worshipped as a war-goddess. She was, moreover, " the woman who sinned before the deluge, the cause of all evil, of all deceit," says one of the old Spanish friars, and who, according to Camargo in his *Historia de Tlaxcalla*, " dwells above the nine heavens in a very pleasant and delectable place, accompanied and guarded by many people, and waited on by other women of the rank of goddesses, where are many delights of fountains, brooks, flower-gardens and without her wanting for anything. . . . But the place where she dwelt was called Tamoanchan, that is, the place where are the flowers the ninefold enchained, the place of the fresh, cool winds." Surely this is the Garden of the Hesperides. The phrase " the ninefold enchained " would seem to point to Atlantis, which, we will recollect, was safeguarded by Poseidon, who constructed round it alternate zones of sea and land. This connects the Ixcuiname not only with the Amazons, but with the Gardens of Hesperides or Atlantis myth, and with the Gorgons, for whoever they looked upon with the evil eye they destroyed. The circumstance that the Ixcuiname came from the coast, and that they introduced a completely new and alien religion into Mexico should not be lost

[1] *La Vérité sur l'Atlantide*, pp. 119–20.

sight of. That they, like the Amazons, were associated
with the serpent is also significant.

But if our theory is to hold water we must also be able
to prove the existence of a similar female cult among the
Guanches of the Canary Islands. Among these there
flourished a sect called the Effenees, who worshipped in
stone circles like the Druids, whose priestesses spoke
oracularly in trance and under hypnotic influence, like the
pythonesses of Greece. These were virgins, and were called
Magades, or Harimagades, over whom presided a high
priest known as Faycan. On the barranco of Valeron the
circle or temple in which they celebrated their peculiar
rites still survives. Like the worshippers of Tlazolteotl,
they engaged in symbolic dances, and in times of national
danger cast themselves into the sea as a sacrifice to the
ocean, which they believed would one day submerge their
islands. Like the priestesses of Tlazolteotl, too, they were
charged with the baptism of infants. Among the Guanches
polyandry was in vogue, and it is clear from their legal
system that a gynecocracy or matriarchal rule obtained
amongst them.

Here then, as in the case of mummification, we have the
clearest evidence of a feminine cult on either side of the
Atlantic, with vestigial traces in the history and traditions
of its islands, both submerged and surviving. If I have
said nothing of witchcraft in the Antilles it is because it
has not yet been proven how much of the great cult of
Obeah which now exists there is African in origin and how
much American. But that powerful American elements
have intermingled with and sophisticated it there can be
no question. In any case, the " bridge " between Europe
and America, so far as the witch or feminine cult is con-
cerned, is obvious enough. It might be formulated :
Aurignacian witchcraft—(Vaulderie or witchcraft, its offshoot, in Southern France and Northern Spain during the
fifteenth and sixteenth centuries)—the Magades of the
Canaries—the Amazons of Africa and the Atlantic island
Hesperia—the Ixcuiname and Ciuateteô of Mexico. The
apostles of what we may, perhaps, call " the Pacific
Route " cannot, I venture to say, bring to the aid of their
fascinating theory—a theory quite legitimate so long as
it does not seek world-wide dominion—any such evidence

as would seem to substantiate the introduction of witch-craft from Asia, where shamanism is almost entirely a masculine institution.

Summarising the evidence, we find that :

(1) A cult of female sorcerers (witchcraft) obtained among the Crô-Magnons, precisely similar to that which existed later in the same era in France and Spain.

(2) That this cult was reflected among the Guanches of the Canary Islands.

(3) That it is to be found in its entirety in Mexico.

(4) That it did not reach America by way of Asia.

(5) That other female cults of the kind (Amazons, Gorgons) are associated with the traditions of the mythical islands of the Atlantic.

(6) That these conclusions traverse the opinions of those who hold that witchcraft is a thing wholly European.

CHAPTER VIII

ETHNOLOGICAL EVIDENCE

AN extraordinary lack of material evidence not-withstanding, little or no dubiety now exists in the minds of the official anthropologists of the United States that the American continent received the greater part of its aboriginal human stock from N.E. Asia, although it is not disputed that throughout the ages emigrants from other sources may have landed on its shores. Not only does America furnish no tangible evidence of antiquity so great as to support the theory of an independent origin for American man, but it has failed so far to afford satisfactory evidence of the arrival of man on the coast in remote geologic times. All American aboriginal culture is classed as Neolithic, and there appears to be no evidence of Palæolithic life from Bering Strait to Tierra del Fuego.

It is assumed that to reach the New World from the Old cultureless man, devoid of fire and clothing, would have required a climate at the point of entrance which would compare with that of Southern California to-day, and even if it could be shown that climatic conditions were favourable at a given period, it would still be necessary to prove that representatives of human stock actually reached and passed the gateway at that period, no matter what other species of mammals accomplished the feat. As will be shown, the failure to discover decidedly early forms of crania in America must be regarded as strong evidence against the arrival of man in the continent in Tertiary or Quaternary time.

Assuming a common place of origin for man in some part of the Old World, America would naturally be the last of the great areas to be reached. If man did reach the American continent by way of Bering Strait it must have been at a comparatively recent period, geologically speaking, for the ice sheet in these regions persisted until an epoch which is variously estimated at from 7000 to 20,000 years ago, and indeed still persists there. His arrival in N.W. America may date from one of the recurring intervals of climatic mildness which intervened during the long and rigorous conditions imposed by the Ice Age. Tribes acclimatised in Siberia would readily make a home in the

Valley of the Yukon, but intervening conditions must have made it difficult for them to reach the Valley of the Columbia, or the St. Lawrence, for many centuries. But migration southward would present no such difficulties, and their spread over the Mississippi Valley to the south would be quickly accomplished, nor would the passage from North to South America present any insuperable obstacles.

In all probability the first settlement of America did not begin until the peoples of Northern Asia had acquired a degree of cultural development somewhat analogous to that of the more primitive hunting, fishing, fire-using tribes of the far north in recent times. Arriving in small groups, the movement would be hesitating and slow. The pioneers would camp along the ocean shores and river courses, and only after a considerable lapse of time would they negotiate the mountain ranges and ice-clad areas. The culture of those who went southward would alter insensibly according to needs and environment, and in time far-reaching changes would be initiated.

After carefully weighing the evidence collected by him in Alaska, Dall reached the conclusion that the earliest midden deposits on the Aleutian Islands are probably about 3000 years old. Indeed the testimony of racial and cultural phenomena when studied apart from geological evidence does not seem to indicate clearly an antiquity for the presence of man in America beyond a few thousand years. On the other hand, the geological evidence of man's presence there would seem to point to occupation towards the close of the last glacial period in middle N. America. This geological evidence is extensive but by no means satisfactory, and in the present state of knowledge it is impossible to accept it as final. Everything points, then, to the conclusion that in all probability America was first peopled by way of Bering Strait at an epoch not less than 7000 and not more than 20,000 years ago.

Since geologic observations were first set on foot a vast body of testimony has been collected regarding man's presence on the continent, and here it is only possible to summarise this rather scantily. South America seems to furnish the most primitive data, and Señor Ameghino and others have sought to push man's antiquity in that sub-

continent back to the early Tertiary Period of the Eocene,
a time when as yet even the anthropoids were not developed. An exhaustive examination of the claims of the
South American School by Dr. Aleš Hrdlička of the U.S.
National Museum and Dr. Bailey Willis of the U.S. Geological Survey left little doubt as to the true character of
its assumptions, which were found to be based on " very
imperfect and incorrectly interpreted data, and in many
instances on false premises."[1] The geologic determinations,
no less than the faulty consideration of the circumstances
relating to the human remains discovered in South America,
particularly as to the possibility of their accidental introduction into older strata, and the lack of anatomical knowledge displayed by the finders, made it clear that even the
best authenticated of their discoveries must be classed as
" doubtful." In the words of Holmes " there appears to
be no very cogent reason for assigning any of the cultural
traces to sources other than tribes occupying the region
in comparatively recent times."

In North America from 1830 onwards a most imposing
body of evidence was gathered to substantiate the claim
for the presence of Tertiary Man, especially in California,
where mining operations resulted in numerous discoveries.
But practically the same disabilities attach to it as to the
South American data. Most of these discoveries were
made by inexpert observers, and it has been demonstrated
that the antiquity claimed for them "required a human
race older by at least one-half than the *Pithecanthropus
erectus* of Dubois." Moreover, they were associated with
artifacts which could certainly not be assigned to the
Tertiary Period, and the knowledge that the western half
of the North American coast has been completely re-
modelled, geologically speaking, twice or three times since
that period at once disabuses such claims of all authenticity.
Still, as Holmes admits, " certain portions of the deep
gravels appear to have yielded traces of human occupancy
of the region during the formation of these deposits."
This partial admission does not, however, extend to such
vaunted relics of the Tertiary Period as the famous
Calaveras skull, the Lansing skull and the Nampa image, a

[1] " Early Man in South America," Bulletin 52, Bureau of U.S. Ethnology.

terra-cotta figurine in human form, taken from early Quaternary deposits in Idaho. The crania in question exhibit such striking analogies with those of the historic Indians as to render their ethnological association with these a matter of small dubiety.

The greater number of observations relating to the geological antiquity of man in America are associated with the closing stages of the Glacial Period in the Northern United States. The Glacial Period in America did not close until the retreat of the main body of the ice-sheet beyond the Arctic shores. That retreat was necessarily gradual, so that the terms " Glacial " and " Post-Glacial " apply to different epochs in different American localities. Thus the former nomenclature might be applied to a period in the Ohio or Delaware Valleys estimated at some 20,000 years ago, whilst in the region of the Great Lakes it refers to an antiquity only half as extensive. The confused and unconsolidated nature of Post-Glacial deposits in North America adds enormously to the difficulties attending an estimate of their age. Man and beast, no less than the forces of nature, have been continuously active in disturbing the superficial strata nor can the geological chronology of the Old World be accepted as a trustworthy guide in any estimate of American geology. In the case of the Tertiary gravels in the Delaware Valley it was proved that the Lenni Lenape Indians had worked certain sites as lately as 1700. This notwithstanding, there can be no question that men have dwelt in the Delaware Valley probably from the closing period of the American Ice Age, but the collection of evidence of their presence there is sadly hampered by the recent existence of the Stone Age in America.

" Thus far," remarks Holmes, " the testimony brought forward is scattered, disconnected and contradictory, and tells no consistent story."[1] He adds that in his view man did not reach American soil " until after the first retreat of the glacial ice from middle North America." So far no definite evidence has been gathered which seriously militates against this conclusion, and until archæological data of a thoroughly trustworthy nature is forthcoming it

---

[1] See Dr. H. Holmes, " Handbook of Aboriginal Antiquities," Bulletin 60, U.S. Bureau of Ethnology, pt. I, *passim*.

must serve as a basis for all estimates of the first presence of man in America.

These views have naturally been combated, chiefly by Mr. Franz Boas, who formulated the dissenting opinion that man reached the American North-west during an Inter-Glacial Period. The 10,000 or 20,000 years which Holmes permits seemed to him sufficient for the growth of American culture, but he pointed out that the ice retreated very gradually from the connecting bridge across the Bering Sea. In fact it still lingers there, so that a much more recent date must be found for the opening of communication by that route. This leaves a very narrow margin for the development of aboriginal culture, and Boas and his supporters assume that the peopling of the New World was contemporaneous with that of Western Europe, and that the subsequent return of the ice practically isolated the two hemispheres, leaving each to develop as it might. They point to a certain parallelism between Western Europe and Eastern North America, and to the fact that European Crô-Magnon man bears in his disharmonic face one of the most prominent of New World characteristics. " More than once," says Clark Wissler, " attention has been called to certain vague similarities between certain Palæolithic races and the Eskimo, and in the New World certain older skulls from the remoter parts of South America are not far removed from this same Eskimo type. Incidentally, we may note that the Chancelade skeleton in Western Europe, belonging to Magdalenian time, is quite similar to the modern Eskimo. The earlier races appearing in Europe tend to be long-headed, and we have noted a less marked but still noticeable tendency for the long-heads in the New World to cluster in the extreme margins. That this is rather fundamental appears when we regard mammals as a whole, for we read that ' when the parallel series in Europe and North America are sufficiently complete, they are seen to be not parallel phyla of local evolution, but periodically recruited by more progressive new stages, apparently from a common centre of dispersal. The relations are like those of one side and the other of a branching tree whose trunk-region is unknown to us.' The human phenomena we have been considering appear, therefore, as but an integral part of

Plate X.—STATUE
Showing Maya type of face, Copan.

mammalian expansion, and, for that reason, become more evident."[1]

Other writers believe that future archæological research in Asia will provide grounds for the assumption that Crô-Magnon man and contemporaneous New World peoples were collateral branches springing from a Central Asian type. Mr. Wissler sums up by inferring that "suggestive parallels between earlier types of Western Europe and America arise in a much earlier period of man's history. That the New World native is a direct descendant of the Asiatic Mongolian is not to be inferred, for the differentiation is evidently remote ; what is implied is that somewhere in the distant past the Asiatic wing of the generalised type diverged into strains, one of which we now know as Mongolian and another as American."

On the other hand some of the younger anthropologists have sought to treat the whole matter independently and *de novo*. Nelson, working in the Mammoth Cave district of Kentucky, found two cultures, the earlier of which is without pottery and with very little polished stone. Spier, making an independent study of conditions at Trenton, New Jersey, found conclusive evidence of the existence of an earlier culture, also without pottery or polished stone. Both of these sites are east of the Mississippi River, and it may therefore be concluded that the existence of two cultural periods in the Eastern United States is extremely probable. " This treatment of remains and artifacts by objective comparison," says Wissler, " permits of chronological distinctions with time-relations being arrived at by analysis, and is, in effect, the soundest of archæological methods, even if it has no starting-point and does not admit of chronological comparison with Old World remains."

Archæological evidence for early European penetration is not lacking, according to Holmes. In New England and farther north is found a highly specialised form of the stone adze known as the gouge, which is abundant in the region mentioned, but disappears as we approach the Carolinas and the Ohio Valley. It is to be found in

[1] *The American Indian*, p. 319. See also Boas, " The History of the American Race," *Annals, New York Academy of Science*, Vol. 21, pp. 177–183.

Northern Europe, where the Atlantic is narrowest and most nearly bridged by intervening islands. Within the same area in North-east America, and thinning out, as does the gouge, to the South and West, is to be found an object of rare and highly specialised form, an axe-like implement known as the hammer-stone, with a perforation for hafting, and wing-like blades. In Northern Europe is found a drilled axe of similar type. It is, says Nilsson, exactly like the axe which the Amazons are represented as carrying in many friezes and statues, and resembles the *"Amazonia securis"* of Horace, which is also mentioned by Xenophon in the " Anabasis." Its American homologue, says Holmes, had no other than sacred and ceremonial functions. " It may not be amiss to suggest that possibly in prehistoric times examples of this type of implement were carried by some voyager across the intervening seas, and that being regarded by the natives as possessed of supernatural attributes these were adopted as ' great medicine.' " Holmes also indicates Mediterranean cultural affinities in America. " Along the middle Atlantic shores of America," he says, " certain forms of artifact are found which resemble more closely the corresponding fabrications of the Mediterranean region than do those of other parts of America. The round-sectioned, petaloid polished celt is found in highest perfection in Western Europe, and in the West Indies and neighbouring American areas. It is absent or rare on the opposite shores of the Pacific. In the Isthmian region we find works in gold and silver and their alloys which display technical skill of exceptional, even remarkable, kind, and it is noteworthy that the method of manufacture employed, as well as some of the forms produced, suggest strongly the wonderful metal-craft of the Nigerian tribes of old Benin ; and, as possibly bearing on this occurrence, we observe that the trade winds and currents of the Atlantic are ever ready to carry voyagers from the African shores in the direction of the Caribbean Sea."

Again the close resemblance between the architectural and sculptural remains of Middle America and South-eastern Asia invite comparison. In both regions the salient structures are pyramids ascended by four steep stairways of stone, bordered by serpent balustrades, and surmounted by temples. The walls of temples are embellished with a profusion of carved ornaments and surrounded by roof-combs of very similar design, and the caryatid is common to both environments. It does not seem impossible that the energetic builders of Cambodia and Java of 2000 years ago should have had sea-going craft capable of the voyage to America. That they had in the sixth century A.D. we know. But by that era Central American civilisation was already on the wane. The polished bronze axes of Cochin China and Cambodia have their exact counterparts in South America, and the stone adzes and pestles of the North-west coast resemble those of the Pacific Islands more closely than they do the corresponding tools of the eastern shores of America. The peculiar flat-bodied stone club or *mere* of Samoa is distributed along the American Pacific coast, and Professor J. Macmillan Brown of Christchurch has recently indicated the basic resemblance between the masonry of Easter Island and that of the Incan Peruvians.

That American civilisation owed its inception to Polynesian immigration is a theory which recommends itself to a growing number of adherents. Perhaps its most direct advocate is Professor J. Macmillan Brown,[1] who sees in the architectural and other manifestations of the Incan culture of Peru a close resemblance to the megalithic culture of Easter Island, and this again he connects with Polynesia, seeing in the hermit isle of the Pacific a stepping-stone by way of which Polynesian arts and beliefs were introduced to American soil. He indicates that the Cyclopean work of some of the burial platforms in Easter Island is precisely the same in character as that to be found at Cuzco in Peru. On the brick-building civilisation of the early Andeans, Professor Brown believes, a stone-building culture borrowed from the Pacific was superimposed by the Incas, who improved and refined it. Professor Brown shows that certain plants which had been acclimatised in Polynesia, the banana and the plantain, the leaves of which are found in Peruvian graves, flourished in South America, and from the presence of the sweet potato he assumes Polynesian influence on the Pacific coast of South America, where the tuber flourished exceedingly.

[1] *Riddle of the Pacific, passim.*

In certain South American customs and forms of artistic endeavour, too, Professor Brown discerns evidences of Polynesian influence. The *tiputa* or *poncho*, the mantle with a single hole for the head, which is so generally worn from Mexico to the Argentine, he believes to be of western insular origin. The salivary ferments common to both areas, *chicha* and *kava*, he compares as having a unity of origin in Polynesian practice, and the chewing of the Andean coca with lime he likens to the practice of masticating the areca nut, which is also chewed with lime in the Pacific. Moreover, the Peruvian *quipos* or system of knotted cords, the purpose of which was to serve as a mnemonic register for facts and numbers and even to supply the first words of songs and chants, he likens to the mnemonic sticks used in Tahiti and among the Maori, who also possessed knotted cords somewhat resembling those in use in Peru. The *umu* or earth-oven of the Pacific also penetrated South America by way of the west coast, and the stone axe or adze of the western insular area was also adopted in the Pacific regions of South America.

Lastly, he infers the arrival of a considerable body of Polynesians on South American soil. Assisted by the Humboldt current, these adventurers landed on the coast near the site of Truxillo, and founded the now ruined city of Grand Chimu, where still stand three doubled-walled enclosures, each covering more than a hundred acres. Within that nearest to the coast are the foundations of many large edifices in front of hundreds of small cubicles, entered only from the roof. These, he believes, were barracks for the soldiery of the conquering intruders, who reserved them as a fortified retreat in the last resort. From the gateway there stretches into the sea about a mile off a weir containing in the middle a dock large enough to accommodate an ocean-going craft, by the aid of which the garrison could if necessary make its escape. But the evidence from which he chiefly identifies the invaders as of Polynesian race is to be found in the cemetery outside the northern wall, in which not a single shard of pottery has been found—for of all the Pacific peoples the Polynesians alone made no pottery, while the native Peruvians lavishly furnished the graves of their dead with ceramic mementoes. A tradition from Lambayeque, an ancient city farther to the north, has it that across the sea came a band of naked warriors who worshipped a god of green stone and who ruled for a time in the neighbourhood and later disappeared.

From what part of Polynesia did these conquering immigrants come ? Professor Brown believes that the settlers in Grand Chimu were no mere haphazard adventurers, but came to Peru as the result of a definite quest for a new home. Searching for other land more or less known, they got into the track of the trades, and were unavoidably blown on to the Pacific coast of South America. He thinks it not improbable that these voyagers came from the Marquesas, where alone in the Pacific area is to be found the combination of megalithic work and statuary reproduced in Incan Peru.

Setting aside the indirect character of much of Professor Brown's evidence, it is obvious that such incursions as he describes could have had but a slight influence on American race and culture. The evidences of Polynesian influence in America are slender, and probably arose out of sporadic visitations such as he describes, visitations which, by reason of the very hostility of the race which made them, could leave but little traces on native art and custom. At the same time it must be admitted that salient and striking customs and artifacts when introduced are usually persistent in character, and to find a highly involved and elaborate form of architecture such as the megalithic in Peru justifies a respectful consideration of the assumption that it emanated from one or other of the Pacific regions where it is to be found.

The argument that America was not only peopled from Polynesia but also drew the seeds of her culture from that region is ably summarised by Mr. Clark Wissler, who says :[1] " Repeated efforts have been made to show that all the higher culture-complexes of the New World were brought over from the Old, particularly from China or the Pacific Islands. Most of these writings are merely speculative or may be ignored, but some of the facts we have cited for correspondences to Pacific Island culture have not been satisfactorily explained. Dixon has carefully reviewed this

[1] Op. cit., 356.

subject, asserting in general that among such traits as
blowguns, plank canoes, lime-chewing, head-hunting cults,
the man's house and certain masked dances common to
the New World and the Pacific Islands, there appears a
tendency to mass upon the Pacific side of the New World.
This gives these traits a semblance of continuous distribution with the Island culture.   Yet it should be noted that
these traits, as enumerated above, have in reality a sporadic distribution in the New World, and that there are
exceptions.   On the other hand, there is no great *a priori*
improbability that some of these traits did reach the New
World from the Pacific Islands."

The several routes possible to immigrants are the Bering
approach, that by way of the mid-Atlantic currents, setting
from the African coast to the shores of South America, the
middle and South Pacific currents traversing the ocean
which separates Polynesia from South America, the Japan
currents setting to the north-east, and the chain of islands
connecting Europe with Labrador.   The majority of these
are certainly not very practicable for primitive voyagers,
but there are numerous instances on record of Polynesian
canoes drifting for six or eight hundred miles from their
point of departure, and of Japanese junks stranded on the
Pacific coast.   Such voyagers as these carried, however,
can scarcely have affected blood and culture to any great
extent in regions already occupied, though there seems to
be good evidence that they did so in some degree.

But even the Bering route has its difficulties.   There is
an interval of forty miles across a tempestuous sea, and it
does not seem probable that a primitive type of man could
have negotiated such a passage.

We have seen that Boas, and to some extent Wissler and
even Holmes admit a certain cultural if not racial connection between European and American man, and that some
of these writers even hint at a definite racial relationship
between Crô-Magnon and American man.   But it is no part
of my thesis to attempt to show that the American race
came exclusively from Asia, Europe, or anywhere else.
From what has gone before, I think I have made it plain
that I regard the Atlantean-Antillian influence which
reached the American continent as having been brought
thither by a relatively small number of refugees from sub-

PLATE XI. — *Top.* AURIGNACIAN FIGURE.
From wall-painting, Alpera, showing likeness to Maya type.

Bottom. TERRA COTTA MASK.
From Sesal, Central America, showing likeness to European type.

merging Antillia—a cultural aristocracy rather than a horde of immigrants.

Many circumstances support this view. The sudden and unheralded appearance of Maya civilisation, a culture without roots in the soil of America, the physical type of the Maya themselves, the persistence of the legends attached to their coming, all serve to show that a comparatively small but enlightened wedge of newcomers was abruptly introduced into Guatemala from some oceanic region to the east of that country.

The non-American character of the art, architecture and science of this people, their non-American physical appearance and the insistence of native tradition that they arrived in the country as strangers and culture-bringers provide the best of proof that the Maya were not only the heirs of Atlantean culture, but that they introduced its arts and customs into the American continent. In another chapter I have dealt with the question of art and architecture and their inter-relations in Europe and America, and the traditions connected with the arrival of the Maya have been exhaustively reviewed. Let us now briefly examine the physiological evidence.

" Briefly," because I do not place such a degree of confidence in it as in the cultural and traditional evidence. Experience has led me to be wary in drawing conclusions as to racial relationships even from data seemingly the most trustworthy. Generally speaking, however, the Maya bear little or no resemblance to the other American Indian tribes. The homogeneity of these from Alaska to Tierra del Fuego is striking, and numerous trusted observers have given it as their opinion that the type of American man, from the far North to the almost Antarctic South, is one and the same. But the Maya Indian of the pre-Columbian period, and even the Maya of to-day, mixed though the stock has been with Carib, negro and white, shows but little physical resemblance to the remainder of the American race.

It is from the numerous sculptures of Guatemala and Yucatan and from the native manuscripts that we obtain the most authentic portraits of the Maya race. In these we observe the following general physical characteristics : flattening of the head by the application during infancy of

K

the cradle-board, so that in later life it slopes backward and exhibits a high and receding forehead ; face oval, with high cheek-bones, nose salient, occasionally almost " Semitic " in shape, in other examples definitely Roman ; eye large and not Mongolian in shape ; body full and bulky ; thighs stout, and in many cases almost exaggerated in appearance ; hair thick on the scalp, and scanty beard not uncommon. In height and weight the Maya probably head the list among the aboriginal peoples of America.

If one compares this with the typical Red Man—and, from the homogeneity of the race, we may fairly assume a typical Red Man—the basic difference between the races will at once become apparent. In the Maya there is a lack of the sinewy development of the Indian. The eye-orbits are considerably larger, and the osseous structure has marked points of dissimilarity to that of the Red Man.

Again, there is little or no resemblance between the historic costumes of the types. The Maya feather head-dress is nothing more or less than the panache of the ancient Aurignacian of Spain, as seen in a painting from Alpera. The men depicted in the cave-painting in question might well pass for typical Maya, judging from their head-gear. This implies that a definite type of head-dress or feather-plume passed from Europe to America. That the Maya feather head-dress was distributed from Central America throughout North America is known. Indian types are never depicted in early European pictures of American aborigines as wearing elaborate feather head-dresses, but a single feather only. The elaborate panache is of late introduction from Central America. The feather panache was distinctly a Maya thing, that is to say, an Aurignacian thing, as were Maya art, Maya symbolism and hieroglyphs and Maya customs.

The cranial distortion or head-flattening practised by the Maya race seems to have been a part of the specific culture which spread from Atlantis to Biscay on one hand and on the other to America. At least we find it among the Basques of Biscay in France and Spain, in the Antilles and on the American mainland, though I cannot trace it in the Canary Islands. Sir Daniel Wilson says that Dr. Foville, " a distinguished French physician at the head of

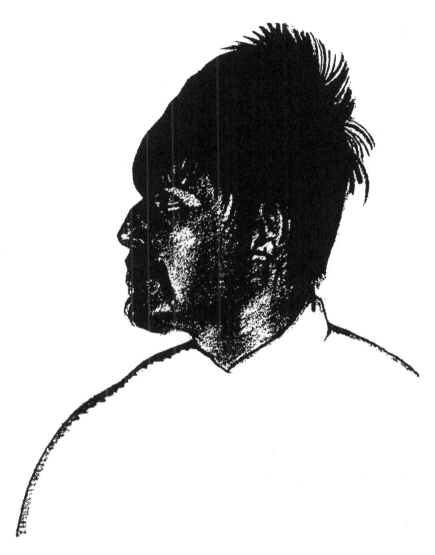

PLATE XII.—PURE AZTEC TYPE.
Showing head-flattening by the cradle-board.

PLATE XIII.—DESIGN ON A VASE.

From Chamá, Central America, showing Maya types.

the Asylum for the Insane in the department of Seine-Inférieure and Charenton, has brought to light the remarkable fact that the practice of distorting the skull in infancy still prevails in France, by means of a peculiar head-dress and bandages ; and in his large work on the Anatomy of the Nervous System, he has engraved examples of such compressed heads, one of which might be mistaken for a Peruvian sepulchral relic. The practice is probably one inherited from times of remote antiquity, and is found chiefly to characterise certain districts. Normandy, Gascony, Limousin and Brittany are specially noted for its prevalence, with some local variations as to its method and results." It is also well known that deformation of the cranium is to-day widely practised by the Basques who occupy almost the same territory as did the Crô-Magnons in Aurignacian times.

As regards cranial deformation among the Indian population of the West Indies, Charlevoix says of the Haitians in his *Histoire de l'Isle Espagnole,* "They flattened their heads by art, thus reducing the size of their forehead, which pleased them greatly. To do this their mothers took care to hold them tightly pressed between their hands or between two little boards, which, by degrees, flattened the head, whereby the skull hardened in a moulded shape."

Francisco Thamara mentions that "they have narrow foreheads, made so artificially by pressure on the sides of the head." This is corroborated by Professor W. K. Brooks and other writers.

A vase from Chamà in Central America depicts several Maya types which closely resemble Crô-Magnon man both in face and figure—the large eye orbits, the high degree of cranial capacity, the salient nose, the heavy and bulky frame. These Maya faces strikingly resemble the " restorations " of Crô-Magnon man's features made by modern sculptors taking as the basis of their work crania found in Aurignacian sites.

Thus in art, beliefs, custom and race we find close analogies between Crô-Magnon man, the Man of Atlantis and the Maya of Central America. The latter, in short, appear to be merely a later form of the Crô-Magnon type, which, during the many centuries which intervened between

Aurignacian and Maya times had undergone special racial and social development, and had after its entrance to America become more or less mingled with the aboriginal races. At the same time certain early South American crania appear to indicate very definitely that bodies of immigrants with Crô-Magnon affinities had entered the American continent ages before the Maya set foot on it, and that this Crô-Magnon blood is largely displayed in the Red Man of North America few candid anthropologists or anatomists will deny.

CHAPTER IX

THE EVIDENCE FROM ART AND ARCHITECTURE

IF, as I have attempted to show in the previous chapter, the Maya were of Crô-Magnon or allied race, one would expect to find their art-forms, although greatly developed because of the lapse of time separating them from Aurignacian types, still bearing the basic resemblance to those types by which it would be possible to trace both to a common source. It is, of course, necessary to realise that artistic developments did not proceed in the ancient world with the rapidity which has marked the evolution of painting in recent centuries. Those developed at no greater rate than did mechanical and scientific processes until the beginning of last century. But I have already laid stress on the point that all trustworthy critics of Aurignacian art have perceived in it no mere crude essaying of savage draughtsmen or sculptors, but a highly developed system of craftsmanship which approaches very nearly to the excellences of the world's greatest artistic triumphs, and as greatly surpasses the flat and spiritless work of the Egyptian and Babylonian schools as it is obvious that a free and untrammelled school of idealists gifted with vision and acute observation must surpass a merely conventional cult trudging along the beaten paths of base imitation—or, shall we say, as a school of archæologists, each member of which is capable of thinking for himself, is bound in the end to outstrip the efforts of official orthodoxy which pins its faith to the tape-measure and eschews all empiricism.

We have already seen that Osborn alludes to the makers of Aurignacian art as " the Palæolithic Greeks." "Artistic observation and representation and a true sense of proportion and beauty were instinctive with them from the beginning . . . their art shows a continuous evolution and development from the first, animated by a single motive, namely the appreciation of beauty of form and the realistic representation of it." Some of it " resembles the work of modern Cubists ? "

Let us briefly examine Aurignacian sculpture, painting and engraving, and the corresponding examples in Maya art, and see how far these bear any resemblances as regards their basic qualities. Aurignacian sculpture is confined to

the human form, usually the female form undraped. Anatomical details are usually exaggerated in the early stages,
and exhibit cleverness, if not finish. In this class may be
placed the female figure from Le Mas d'Azil sculptured
from the tooth of a horse (the face is distinctly " Maya "
in type) and the statuette in ivory from Brassempouy,
depicting a woman with exaggerated female characteristics.
The farthest eastern example of this class comes from
Willendorf, is carved in limestone, and the treatment of
the pendant breasts strongly resembles those seen in the
statue of a goddess found in Mexico City.

At Laussel in the Dordogne several remarkable sculptures in relief have been discovered. One representing a
man might well be the prototype of many early Maya
forms.

In early Aurignacian painting, says Macalister,[1] " the
oldest remains are not human figures, but human hands,
which are traced upon the walls of certain caves by the
following method : a hand was pressed against the wall
and colouring matter projected upon it, either with the
other hand or by expulsion from the mouth of the artist.
The process finished, the hand would be left silhouetted,
or rather stencilled, upon the wall. The most remarkable
series of such hands exists in the cave of Gargas, Hautes-
Pyrenees. . . . A very curious feature of the Gargas hands
is the mutilation of the fingers which they display. In
many of them the fingers have almost disappeared. This
has been explained as (a) evidence for the prevalence of a
mutilating disease, such as leprosy ; (b) evidence for a
custom of finger-lopping, a form of mutilation found among
nature-folk in several quarters of the modern world ; and
(c) as merely the result of bending the fingers in the process
of stencilling. The third hypothesis may be excluded, as
the flexibility of a pianist's fingers would be needed in
some cases, and in others the bending postulated is impossible. The first is improbable. There are sufficient
analogies for the second to make it the most likely explana-
tion. It is to be noticed that the hands at Castillo and at
Font-de-Gaume do not display these mutilations."[2]

Now this practice we find duplicated in many parts of

[1] *A Text-book of European Archæology*, p. 455.
[2] *Ibid.*, p. 458.

America. During the period of mourning among the Crow Indians, says Beckworth, "fingers were dismembered as readily as twigs." Slaves in Mexico before sacrifice stencilled their hands on the door-posts of their captors.

During the Magdalenian or middle stage of Aurignacian art human gave place to animal sculpture. The Espelungues horse and the superb head of a horse from Mas d'Azil are worthy of Athens in her prime, as is the marvellous series of relief sculptures discovered in the rock-shelter at Cap Blanc, near Laussel, which depict a procession of horses. Detail now begins to show itself in engraving, the first signs of that luxuriance which was to flower so superabundantly in Maya sculpture. Animal forms became increasingly numerous. Among these the bison wellnigh predominates, just as he does in the art of the Plains Indians. Says Macalister (p. 479) : "Some of these marks or groups of marks have been claimed as proving the astonishing theory that Magdalenian man had evolved a form of writing by symbolic signs. But such a thesis cannot be sustained. The records of hunting expeditions and of similar events found among American Indians and other nature-folk, which have been adduced in corroboration, tend rather to disprove than to support it." The general resemblance between what may be called the "animal" stage in Aurignacian art and that of the North American Indian hunting tribes is indeed much too close to be fortuitous. Compare the pictures of a stag and buffalo hunt from Cogul with the drawing taken from the book of an Indian prisoner at St. Augustine, representing the same thing, or the Aurignacian wall-painting at Alpera depicting a great hunt with the petroglyph at Millsboro, Pennsylvania. If these do not spring from the same artistic sources then there is no resemblance between any two forms in the whole range of art.[1]

To come now to Maya art and its associations with Aurignacian forms. It is of course essential to turn to motifs. The most important is the mammoth motif.

The mammoth is very frequently pictured in Aurignacian art, as in the statuette found at Predmost and else-

[1] See Macalister, op. cit., pp. 495 and 497, and Dollenbaugh, *The North American Indians of Yesterday*, pp. 43 and 61.

where. And as the accompanying illustrations show, mammoths, and art-forms derivative of them, are frequent enough in Maya art. The theory that the form of the prehistoric elephant is reflected in Maya art differs from that of Professor Elliot Smith[1] (who believes the Asian elephant to be depicted in certain sculptures at Copan), in that it supposes such representations in Central America to be memories of the Atlantic elephant. Plato says most emphatically that the elephant was a native of Atlantis, and doubtless the ancient Maya sculptors had handed down to them the memory of these Atlantean elephants. The so-called elephant gods with mammoth characteristics were *invariably associated with the eastern point of the compass,* and not with the west. Thus God B, as he is usually called, an " elephant-headed " god, who is probably Quetzalcoatl, is associated, says Schellhas, with the signs of the east, and as Quetzalcoatl is, of course, also associated with the mystic western land of Tlapallan in the Atlantic. He carries Quetzalcoatl's peculiar perforated staff, the Caluac, and is connected with the Tree of Life, another Atlantean or Hesperidean symbol. God K, another deity with an elephant-like head, is regent or lord of the Ben group of years belonging to the east, and has rightly been identified by Förstemann as a deity of the storm, and by Seler as a god of water and the ocean. So it is self-evident that these elephant-like divinities were associated in the minds of the Maya with the east and the Atlantic rather than with the west and the Pacific. It seems to me much more reasonable to conjecture that they are the memories of Atlantean mammoths rather than of Asiatic elephants. The elephant or mammoth motif has abundant illustration in the architecture of Central America.

Another Aurignacian memory seems to be exhibited in the frequent representation of human bones in Maya sculpture and drawing, both as ear ornaments and textile patterns. These recall the preservation and painting of the bones of Crô-Magnon man, a custom which we have seen spread widely throughout the American continent. Spinden comments on the extraordinary figuring of the bone motif in Maya art.[2]

If we pass to a consideration of the shell ornaments of

[1] See his *Elephants and Ethnologists,* 1924.　　[2] *Maya Art,* p. 85.

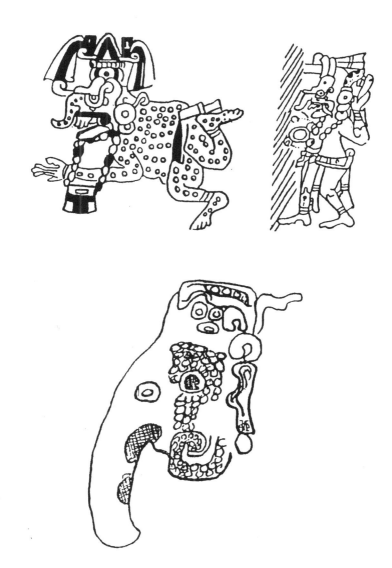

The elephant-headed god.
The mammoth or elephant at Copan.

the American races we will find some curious parallels with Aurignacian practice.

Macalister tells us that Aurignacian Man was buried " possibly in wrappings of hides, and certainly in elaborate ornaments, presumably of leather, into which devices of shells had been sewn. These shells covered the heads and the breasts. In addition there were necklets, armlets, anklets, and girdles of shells, fish vertebræ and teeth of animals."[1] Most of the shells he says were " perforated for suspension as ornaments, either singly or grouped in collars or similar decorations. The holes were made in different ways. Sometimes a saw-cut was made in the shell surface, by means of a flint flake, to reduce the shell wall to perforable dimensions, a flint needle being then thrust through the remainder. Sometimes the saw-cut was absent, the hole being drilled from the first ; and sometimes the face of the shell was ground flat by being rubbed over a rough surface, the perforation being then drilled through the wall of the shell, thus reduced to a convenient thinness."[2]

Now this is precisely the manner in which American wampum was manufactured. Wampum, as its name implies, is manufactured from beads laboriously ground from various species of shells, either clam, periwinkle or whelk, though beads made from other and fresh-water species are to be found in collections.

The process of manufacture was involved, and demanded careful manipulation and long practice. The wampum made on the Atlantic seaboard was either white or purple, the white manufactured from the periwinkle shell being the more common, and the darker shade, which was more esteemed, from the blue portion of the clam shell. First the thin portions of the shell were removed with a light hammer, then the tougher remaining portion was clamped in a split stick and ground into an octagonal shape. It was then firmly secured to a bench by a heavy weight, and then drilled lengthwise by a bow-drill braced against a plate held on the operator's chest. From a vessel suspended over the drill drops of water fell to lessen the friction, which otherwise would have caused the shell to

[1] Macalister, *A Text-book of European Archæology*, p. 512.
[2] *Ibid.*, p. 526.

split. The beads were then polished and hung on hempen strands or twine made of gut, about a foot in length.

Beverley, in his *History of the Indians*, says that those of the Virginia and Carolina seaboard had two varieties of wampum, *peak* and *roanoke*. The peak was of two colours, dark purple and white, which were alike in size and made from different parts of the same shell. They also manufactured from the same substance what he calls *runtees*. These were either large, like an oval bead, drilled through the length of the oval, or they were flat and circular, nearly an inch in width and one-third of an inch thick, and drilled edgewise. Roanoke was made from the cockleshell, which was broken into small fragments with the edges left rough, and drilled through it in the same manner as the other shell beads.

But wampum was also made by the prehistoric men of America. For this statement we have the authority of the late M. H. Beuchat, who writes : " L'usage de la coquille de grands univalves (*Busycon perversum*) comme coupes à boire paraît avoir été général dans les regions du Sud. Peut-être les nombreuses coquilles de cette espèce trouvées dans les mounds ont-elles servi à cet usage, et il est probable que les restes très nombreux d'*Unio* qu'on y trouve étaient des cuillers. Mais les objets de coquille travaillés sont presque tous des ornements. Les perles y sont très abondantes. Les plus simples sont faites de petites coquilles d'univalves (*marginella, oliva, cypres*) perforées. Une autre variété très commune est la perle en forme de bouton, plaque circulaire découpée dans un test de coquille et percée d'un trou au centre. Il existe aussi en quantites considérables des perles cylindriques, faites de la columelle de certains mollusques univalves ; ces cylindres, de coleur blanche, pourpre ou noire, ressemblent complètement à ceux dont les Indiens du Canada et de la Nouvelle-Angleterre faisaient leurs wampums."

It would seem then that the manufacture of this " wampum " was an art which Aurignacian Man had in common with prehistoric and historic American Man. Shell ornaments are found elsewhere, but not wampum.

The architectural form by which the art of Africa is chiefly linked to that of America is the pyramid. Where did the pyramid originate, and what is its significance—and is that significance the same in America as in Africa ?

That the pyramid was evolved out of the idea of the sacred hill appears as the most probable solution of the mystery underlying its origin. In early Egypt, Mexico and Peru certain hills and mountains were regarded as especially sacred, and were even regarded as totemic or tribal lodges. These eminences were looked upon as the homes of powerful supernatural beings, and sometimes as the places of origin of the clan or tribe. We have seen that the mountain is clearly associated with the tradition of Atlantis, both in Plato's account and in those American legends which seem to refer to Atlantean circumstances. The mountain in Mexico is in many cases a kind of natural pyramid, the dwelling of the goddess of fertility, just as it was her altar. In the more civilised portions of the western continent it was faced with stone, like the Egyptian pyramid, but in what is known as the region of the Mound-Builders it is constructed from earth alone. The link between the Mexican pyramid constructed from masonry and the simple earthen hill is provided by the earthen mound sacred to the goddess Coatlicue close to the teocalli or pyramid of her son Uitzilopochtli at Mexico, and intended to represent the sacred hill near Tollan where she was supposed to dwell.

Persons of importance were buried in these hills, the act, it was believed, placing their remains under the especial protection of the genius or divinity of the height. From the mountains it was thought, both in America and Egypt, the sun proceeded on his rising. Thus from the mountain near Tollan which was identified with Coatlicue it was thought her son Uitzilopochtli was reborn each day as the sun, and certain Egyptian pyramids are alluded to in some texts as " the mountain of Ra," the height from which the sungod rose every morning.

The earliest Mexican pyramids were mere masses of earth or adobe raised in imitation of the sacred hill. The first Egyptian pyramids were likewise built of earth, for the Nile mud from which they were constructed bakes so naturally into brick by the heat of the sun alone that it can scarcely be regarded as other than the natural soil. American and Egyptian pyramids have thus a common

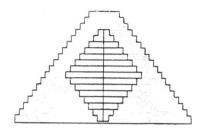

Plate XIV — AMERICAN PYRAMIDS

Top: Plan of Peruvian pyramid

Bottom: Maya form of pyramid

evolutionary history. Both would appear to trace their descent to the sacred hill of Atlantis mentioned by Plato, which, according to Mrs. M. A. Blackwell, has similar dimensions to those of the pyramid of Xochicalco in Mexico.

Plato tells us that this sacred hill was a " low mountain " at a distance of fifty stadia from the centre of the island. This height the god Poseidon enclosed with zones of sea and land to ensure its sanctity. This " low mountain " I take to be the prototype of both the American and the Egyptian pyramid. I may once more be permitted to draw attention to the extraordinary resemblance between the names of the goddesses who presided over the Atlantean and Mexican sacred hills respectively—Cleito and Coatlicue—whose respective sons were Atlas and Uitzil, both twin brothers, both mountain-born, both the supporters of the world, and with many other points of contact and resemblance.

Do we find similar mythic circumstances connected with the pyramid in Egypt ? The goddess Isis, wife of Osiris, is, like Coatlicue, a goddess of fertility. On her head she wears the ideogram of her name (explained as meaning " the House of Osiris "), which is obviously a pictograph of a hill or high place crowned by a shrine. " The House of Osiris " can mean little else than " pyramid," for Osiris was a " dead " god, and was thought of as reclining in his pyramid tomb. Horus, the son of Osiris and Isis, is a figure almost identical with the Mexican Uitzilopochtli. Like him, Horus is a sun-god, he is depicted as having a bird's head, he is a mighty warrior, and, like Uitzilopochtli, the avenger of his mother. Like the Cabiri, he is connected with smith-work and the lance. Moreover, human sacrifice was associated with the early phases of the cult of Horus, as it was with the cult of the Mexican Uitzilopochtli, for when he took prisoner the followers of his enemy Set, he bound them with chains and slaughtered them one by one on a later occasion. The followers of Horus were a caste of sun-worshippers, and human blood was as necessary to the sustenance of the sun in early Egypt as it was in ancient Mexico, where the military caste, living under the patronage of the sun, always refrained from slaying an enemy in battle if they could make him prisoner, to be sacrificed at leisure. We seem then to have in Egypt a counterpart of what may be called the " pyramid complex " in Mexico—a mother goddess and son, typifying the mountain and the sun which arises therefrom, and associated with the pyramid and burial of the mummified dead.

It is also not a little remarkable that Set is placed in the North in opposition to Horus in the South, just as Tezcatlipoca is to Uitzilopochtli. Set and Tezcatlipoca are both associated with the North, with the constellation of the Great Bear, and with darkness, cold and death, and both are alike the deities of the darker side of magic and necromancy.

Now if our theory of a pyramid culture-complex in the region of Atlantean culture be correct we shall find pyramids in the Canaries and the Antilles. According to M. Gattefossé, we do find them in the Canaries. He says : " Quelquefois aussi, des *tumuli* en forme de pyramide étaient formés au-dessus du cadavre placé sur des tréteaux, la tête dirigée vers le Nord. D'autres pyramides paraissent être des exvotos des temples ou des figurations divines ou astronomiques, peut-être à la fois l'un et l'autre, comme chez les Egyptiens ou les Rouges du Mexique. Les catacombes du Baranco de Herquo, decouvertes au temps de Clavija, et celles de Laguna sont bien connues ; les *xaxos* qui en ont été retirées figurent à l'Escurial et dans divers musées."[1]

Moreover, we encounter the pyramid or its prototype in the Antilles, the other insular link between Europe and America. Says Fewkes :[2] " Just outside the boundary wall of every one of the inclosures studied by the author there were found one or more low mounds which bear superficial evidences of having been made by human hands. Excavations near one of these mounds near Utuado were made by the writer in 1903, and a brief reference to the result of his work appears in the following quotation from his account of Porto Rican pictography : In my studies of one of these inclosures at Utuado I found that the main road from that town to Adjuntas had cut through the edge of one of the mounds, revealing, a few feet below the surface, a layer of soil containing fragments of pottery, a few broken celts, and the long bones of an adult. This

[1] *Adam*, p. 94.
[2] *Aborigines of Porto Rico*, p. 82 ff.

discovery induced me to extend a trench diametrically through the mound, parallel with the sides of the inclosure. The depth of this trench, at the middle of the mound, was about 9 feet. The excavation revealed that the mound rested on a hard gravel base and was composed of soil so rich that some of it was carried away by the neighbouring farmer for use as fertilizer. This earth was very moist and ill-adapted to the preservation of bones or other fibrous material. Nevertheless, we found ten skeletons of adults and infants, with mortuary objects so distributed as to indicate that they had been placed there as offerings. One of the best preserved of these skeletons was found in a sitting posture with its legs drawn to its chest and with ceramic objects lying at one side. The frontal bases of the skulls were abnormally flattened, as in those from the caves from the northern part of Santo Domingo, described by Dr. Llenas. The discovery that these mounds are Indian cemeteries sheds light on the nature and use of the neighbouring enclosures. The conclusions drawn from my excavations of the Utuado mounds are that large numbers of the dead were buried just outside the dance courts and that the elaborate *areitos*, or mortuary dances, were held in the latter. There is evidence also of the interment of the dead in caves, human skeletons from the cave at Jobo, near the road from Arecibo to Utuado having been given to me by Dr. Cabello. But the majority of the prehistoric Porto Rican dead were undoubtedly buried in the cemeteries above referred to." We thus find prototypal pyramids in the Antilles associated with the burial of the dead, mortuary dances, the Maya custom of flattening the skull, and, as Fewkes states on a later page, with ancestor-worship.

From Egypt to Peru, then, we find the pyramid associated with the embalmed body. In Mexico and Peru pyramids were employed as burial sites. Near Palenque, in Chiapas, the city of Quetzalcoatl, Waldeck found two pyramids, almost perfectly preserved, pointed at the apex, like those of Egypt, their sides forming equilateral triangles. The Pyramid of the Sun at Teotihuacan, which is alluded to further on, has an opening 69 feet from its base, entering upon a gallery in which it is possible to make progress on hands and knees only. This inclines gently for a distance of 25 feet, ending in two chambers each 5 feet square, obviously intended for the reception of mummies. In describing this gallery Lowenstein remarks that it is " 157 feet long, increasing in height to over 6½ feet as it penetrates the pyramid ; the well is over 6 feet square, extending apparently to the base and up to the summit. Other cross-galleries are blocked by debris." This statement is curiously reminiscent of the description of the interior of the Egyptian Pyramid of Cheops.

It is obvious that these structures and many others to be found over the length and breadth of Mexico and Central America cannot be directly associated with Egyptian influence. It is known that pyramid building did not originate in Egypt, that, indeed, it was not initiated in the Nile country until the period of the IIIrd Dynasty, or about 3000 B.C. Prior to that epoch the graves of the Egyptian kings were mere sand-pits lined with bricks made from Nile mud. The stone or granite pyramid was assuredly introduced by a race from the west who had had experience of the mason's craft elsewhere, the same people who raised the menhirs and dolmens and vast stone circles of Brittany and Britain—the Iberians, the descendants of the Azilian-Tardenoisians, the third wave of Atlantean immigrants to Europe. They have left a clearly defined record of their eastward progress in the monuments they raised *en route*, and it is clear that in the more favourable environment of Egypt their craft took on a form and finish reminiscent of a former type which had been evolved in an equally favourable atmosphere. As in the case of mummification, with which it was associated, the same phenomenon took place in America. Indeed, the early efforts of these wandering stone-masons are to be descried in American dolmens, and the Maya stele is nothing but a highly elaborate development of the more humble menhir or stone shaft which marked the grave of the king or tribal chieftain.

The dolmen, as is generally known, is a large stone upheld by three other great stones and covered with an earthen mound. It is a step either in the evolution or degeneracy of the pyramid. It, too, was employed as a burial chamber, and may, indeed, have been a degenerate form of the original Atlantean pyramid or sacred hill, the memory of which had grown dim among a people who had been separated from the fatherland for generations, and who had lost the mechanical knowledge essential to the raising of great masses of stone—if, indeed, they had ever possessed it. For the Egyptian and Maya pyramids may have been nothing but attempts to reproduce artificially the great traditional sacred hill of their Atlantean fatherland.

Around this sacred hill the entire traditions of the Atlantean emigrants must have clustered. It was their Lebanon, their Sinai, on which stood the temple of their gods, and in the caverns of which, doubtless, the embalmed bodies of the founders of their civilisation, their kings and priests, were preserved.

The area of funerary mounds and pyramids in North America is immense. It extends from the Red River on the North to the Gulf of Mexico in the South, and from the Middle West to the Atlantic. The majority of the mounds in Ohio, Kentucky, Tennessee and elsewhere consist of conical earthen structures of a greater or less altitude. In these funerary mounds, which occur near the north-western limits of the area alluded to, bodies are deposited in a shallow grave, in Ohio and Virginia burial is associated with burning, while in W. Tennessee there exists a peculiar method of mound sepulture, the bodies resting on a floor of half-fired brick and being surrounded by votive objects.

Many of these funerary mounds have been found[1] " to cover a single skeleton : though in one or two exceptional instances in other localities, of which the Grave Creek Mound of Virginia is the most remarkable, more than one body has been deposited under the mound. Numerous as monuments of this class are, their relative numbers, when compared with the sacred and civic works of the same districts, abundantly prove that they are not the common places of sepulture, but monumental memorials of the distinguished dead. They vary in size from 6 to 80 feet in height, but the greater number range from 15 to 25 feet, and frequently occur in groups, where smaller mounds are ranged round one of considerable dimensions." In one of these mounds in the Scioto Valley " traces of a rude sarcophagus or framework of unhewn logs were found, the cast of which still remained in the compacted earth. The

---

[1] Sir Daniel Wilson, *Prehistoric Man*, pp. 358-9, Vol. II.

bottom had been laid with matting or wood, the only remains of which were a whitish stratum of decomposed vegetable matter; and the timbers once covering the simple sarcophagus had in like manner decayed and allowed the superincumbent earth to fall on the enclosed skeleton."[1]

The majority of these mounds, then, contained but a single corpse, and in this they resemble the Egyptian pyramid and the Mexican teocalli.

In North Carolina the system of inhumation was to make an excavation in triangular form 2 or 3 feet deep, in which the corpse was deposited. Over this was raised a small pyramid of earth. In Ohio and Western Virginia skeletons have been found buried in coffins of wood or stone covered by heaped stones. In Illinois, Kentucky and Tennessee stone cists or coffins are numerous. Some of the bodies were placed on stone slabs or tables, reminiscent of the slab of the mummifier, and others were disposed round a given centre in a radiating manner. Many of these bear traces of having been partially consumed by fire, so that embalmment must have been followed by partial cremation as a concession to local religious practice and belief—a strange mingling of the two processes of mummification and cremation, exhibiting a very marked condition of culture-mixing, or the opposition and subsequent blending of two distinct racial cultures, immigrant and native.

In the Mississippi region two types of funerary mound are met with—one a simple tumulus of earth mingled with stones or composed entirely of stone, thus exhibiting stages in the development or degeneration of the idea of the pyramid or sacred hill. In the stone mounds the bodies are found enclosed in stone coffins, while in those composed of soil alone they have been cremated. The latter examples are probably those of a race of less culture, who copied in earth the stone erections of a people of higher advancement.

Literally thousands of pyramids or earthen mounds not employed for funerary purposes are also to be found on

---

[1] For a general discussion of the pyramidal mounds of North America, see W. H. Holmes, "Aboriginal Pottery of the United States," Bulletin 20 of the U.S. Bureau of Ethnology, and Cyrus Thomas, *Introduction to the Study of North American Archæology.*

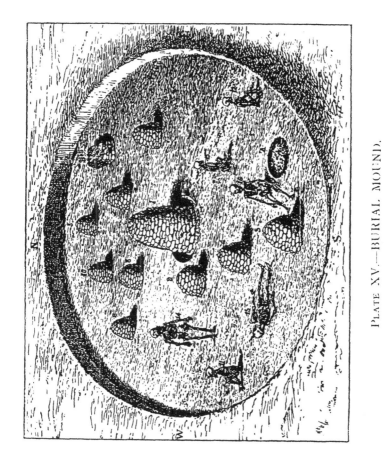

PLATE XV.—BURIAL MOUND.

In Caldwell County, N. Carolina (after C. Thomas, "Mound Explorations.")

North American soil. These are the erections of a race
called by archæologists "the Mound Builders." The
real home of the Mound Builders was the basin of the
central and upper Mississippi and its eastern affluents,
especially the Ohio, the groups of such erections lying outside this area being classed as radiations from it. The
Mound Builders have long provided Americanists with an
archæological problem of extraordinary complexity. Indeed the pyramids they built have been associated with
nearly every race, civilised and savage, under the sun.
Their erections stretch into the north near the Great Lakes
and far into the territory of Canada.

" Unquestionably," says Professor Konrad Haebler,
" the artificial mounds were the work of a sedentary race,
for the Indian who roamed about in the state of a nomad
could not possibly have had time, power or inclination to
erect even the most insignificant of these earthworks, not
to speak of the structures—not very numerous, but of
imposing dimensions—of Etowah, Cahokia, etc., the largest
of which had a content of 3,000,000 to 4,000,000 cubic feet.
To erect such structures required a population of far
greater density than had ever been found anywhere on the
North American continent, but one that must have been
excellently organised to be able to subject such labour as
those gigantic works entailed to a common will. But what
a race, what a state must that have been which not only
produced those structures but protected the banks of the
chief river courses for many miles with extensive fortifi-
cations such as would seem in early times to have accompanied the Mississippi in an almost uninterrupted chain
from the mouth of the Arkansas up to the Illinois. And
an almost incredible range of territory is given to this
state if, instead of merely taking into account the region
most thickly covered with such earthworks, we extend its
boundaries as far as the earthworks can be found."

A population of such density as the presence of these
mounds implies must naturally have depended upon an
agricultural mode of life. Indeed this was demonstrated
on the excavation of the mounds, as was the fact that their
builders possessed high skill in the making of pottery and
objects in copper. That they must have had a special
knowledge of architecture was also proved beyond all

doubt by the almost incredible number of earthworks erected by them, for structures were found which reproduced the mathematical figures of the polygon, circle, rectangle and square with an accuracy which investigators pronounced to be quite inconceivable without the use of instruments.

The general opinion is that these vast structures were raised by the ancestors of the present Indians. De Soto, indeed, in the sixteenth century, observed several of them in the occupation of Indian tribes, who employed them as fortresses or places of refuge. This, no doubt, was a legacy to the native tribes from some race of higher culture, but that the Indians of North America conceived the idea of these massive structures in the first instance, or that they developed the architectural skill or invented the instruments necessary to their erection is a notion too grotesque for acceptance.

I believe the Mound Builders of North America to have been the cultured descendants of those Maya-Toltecs who found their way from Guatemala to Mexico, and who, quite conceivably, may have pushed much farther north. Indeed this view is accepted by many authorities of weight. Their structures, indeed, are much too similar to the teocalli pyramids of Mexico not to have had a common origin with these, and when we learn that human sacrifice was occasionally celebrated on their summits, little more proof is required to make it clear that the race which introduced them into the Mississippi region was one and the same with that which raised the horrid pyramids of slaughter to Uitzilopochtli and his brother in Mexico. Like the Mexican and Maya pyramids, the erections of the Mound Builders can scarcely be anything else than reminiscences of the sacred hill of Atlantis. Moreover, just as that eminence was associated with the sacrifice of the sacred bull, so were the pyramids of the Mound Builders associated with the ceremonial slaughter of the buffalo.

At Teotihuacan, in Mexico, the teocallis or pyramids of the sun and moon still stand. The teocalli of the moon has a base covering 426 feet and a height of 137 feet. That of the sun is of greater dimensions, with a base of 735 feet and a height of 203 feet. These pyramids were divided into four stories, three of which remain. On the summit of that of the sun stood a temple containing a great image of that luminary carved from a rough block of stone. In the breast was inlaid a star of the purest gold, seized afterwards as loot by the insatiable followers of Cortes. From the teocalli of the moon a path runs to where a little rivulet flanks the " Citadel." This path is known as " The Path of the Dead," from the circumstance that it is surrounded by some nine square miles of tombs and tumuli, and, indeed, forms a road through the great cemetery. The literature of the subject is extensive— quite as extensive in fact as that of the Egyptian pyramid. There is thus no gap in pyramidical construction between Egypt and America save that of the Atlantic abyss.

The pyramid is thus as much a thing American as a thing Egyptian, which implies that, occurring so far apart as they do, neither form can have originated in the area in which it is found, and that the place of origin must be sought in an intermediate (oceanic) area.

CHAPTER X

FOLK-MEMORIES OF AN ATLANTIC CONTINENT

I HAVE already made it clear that a very definite traditional memory of Atlantis-Antillia lingered among the peoples of Europe until a comparatively recent period, and that the name Antillia was bestowed by them upon the present West India Islands naturally, and as if in the full knowledge that such a locality had always been known to them. Nothing, indeed, is more clear from mediæval maps and traditions than that our forefathers were convinced that certain land-masses occupied the mid-Atlantic. But the idea they entertained regarding these must not in all cases be confounded with the notion of a great western continent. When the continental character of the mainland of America was at last realised, it came to everyone in Europe, learned and unlearned, as a surprise. But the tradition of islands or island-continents lying in the Atlantic had for centuries been current and can only have arisen out of a most ancient certainty that such lands actually existed. In reality, many well-authenticated expeditions set sail with the intention not of discovering but rediscovering these Atlantic localities.

During the Victorian Age the former existence of these mythical islands, or their identification with one region or another, was officially scouted, but of late years much has been done to show that many localities which our grandfathers firmly believed to be fabulous were actually known to European geographers before the dates generally accepted as those of their several discoveries. Many an ancient voyage which was formerly classed with the Odyssey and the cruise of the Argo, has recently been verified by research as having had a well-authenticated existence.

During the nineteenth century the venerable legend of the voyage of St. Brandan was believed to enshrine quite as much of the essence of legend as any other of the Irish sagas of seafaring. The Norse tales of discovery in America were credible enough, but this Celtic epic of the earthly paradise was, of course, much too rich in matter of faery to carry conviction. Perhaps its most acceptable version is that to be found in the fifteenth-century Book of Lismore, compiled from much older materials, from which we learn that St. Brandan, the founder of the monastery of Clonfert, who flourished in the seventh century, prayed strenuously that a secret and hidden land might be shown him where he could dwell in hermitage secure from men. An ancient tradition assures us that he wandered up and down the coast of Kerry " seeking for traditions of the western continent." At first he set sail in search of his earthly paradise in a ship made of the hides of beasts, but later in a large wooden vessel built in Connaught, which required a crew of sixty monks to navigate her. Success crowned his quest, and he came at last to an island " under the lee of Mount Atlas," a balmy and delectable region, where he dwelt in peace and security many years.

The first appearance of St. Brandan's Isle in cartography is in the Hereford map of 1275, where it occupies the latitude of the Canary group. Indeed in the Canary Isles a tradition still survives that St. Brandan and his companions spent several years in the archipelago. Even as late as the eighteenth century an expedition sailed from the Canaries in search of an island believed to be outside of those already known in the group, and to be that on which St. Brandan had settled. " It appears likely," says Mr. W. H. Babcock, " that St. Brandan in the sixth century wandered widely over the seas in quest of some warm island concerning which wonderful accounts had been brought to him, and found several such isles, the Madeira group receiving his especial approval, according to the prevailing opinion of the fourteenth and fifteenth centuries."

But evidence of the most interesting kind is accumulating that the legendary island of Brazil, once thought of as lying in the Atlantic, may actually have been the present Newfoundland, which seems to have been visited at an early period by Irish-speaking people. The name Brazil is probably composed of two Celtic syllables, " breas " and " ail," each highly commendatory in implication. In all probability the Irish monks whom early Norse settlers found in Ireland formed part of a great Celtic and missionary " push," which was pressing northwards and eastwards in the latter part of the eighth century, and the

Irish who reached Newfoundland may have formed its westward wing. Irish vessels at that period were of a tonnage sufficiently large to negotiate such a voyage with safety and success. Indeed they were much better equipped in every respect than the vessels of Columbus. It is well known that the Norse discoverers of America conferred the name of Mikla Irlant, or Great Ireland, on a region not far distant from one of the coasts where they settled. The territory which has Cape Race for its apex, and which includes Newfoundland and Cape Breton Island, occupies the precise latitude of the island of Brazil in many of the ancient maps. The name Brazil was given to the South American country now so called in quite a haphazard manner, and in the vague belief that the legendary locality of that name had been rediscovered after the lapse of centuries.

Brazil is first mentioned in modern literature by William Bettover, called William of Worcester, who says that on July 15th, 1480, his brother-in-law, John Jay, began a voyage from Bristol in search of the island, returning on September 18th without having found it. Pedro Ayala, the Spanish Ambassador to England, mentions in a letter dated 1498 that the mariners of Bristol had made a series of voyages in search of the island, which goes to show that a persistent tradition regarding it must surely have existed.

Hardiman, in his *Irish Minstrelsy or Bardic Remains of Ireland*, which was written about 1636, says that there is an " iland which lyeth far att sea on the west of Connaught, and sometimes is perceived by the inhabitants of the Oules and Iris . . . and from St. Helen's Head. Likewise several seamen have discovered it . . . one of whom, Captain Rich, who lives about Dublin, of late years had a view of the land, and was so neare that he discovered a harbour . . . but could never make to land, because of a mist which fell upon him. Allsoe in many old mappes . . . you still find it by the name of O'Brasile." In 1675 a pretended account of a visit to this island was published in London, which is reprinted by Hardiman.

Of equal importance is the legendary Isle of Seven Cities, which is described as the largest of the islands of the mediæval geographers, and as rectangular in shape, extending from north to south, and lying in mid-Atlantic about latitude 35 degrees north. It appears again and again in the maps of the fourteenth, fifteenth and later centuries, and it was thought before the discovery of America that it might be found suitable as a kind of half-way house to the Indies. The legend states that it was discovered and settled by refugees from Spain in A.D. 714, after the defeat of King Roderic by the Moors. There is also a story that the island was rediscovered by a Portuguese mariner in 1447. Says Ferdinand Columbus, son of the discoverer, " It is not above 200 leagues west of the Canaries and the Azores, and was peopled by the Portuguese at the time when Spain was conquered by the Moors in the year 714. At which time they say seven bishops, with their people, embarked and sailed to this island, where each of them built a city; and to the end, none of their people might think of returning to Spain they burnt the ships, tackle, and all things necessary for sailing. Some Portuguese discoursing about this island, there were those that affirmed several Portuguese had been to it who could not find the way to it again."

Galvano tells of a still later visit to the Isle of the Seven Cities in 1447. But the main point regarding it is that its name is to be found in the Azores at the present time. The island of St. Michael's has still its Valley of the Seven Cities. Formerly some ruins were to be seen at this spot, but only fragments of them are now visible.

There is the best of evidence that the island of Buss, another insular locality which achieved legendary fame at a later date, was actually discovered by English sailors in 1578. Best, writing of Frobisher's third voyage in that year, says that one of his vessels, a buss, or small fishing craft, of Bridgewater, called the *Emmanuel*, made the discovery. He says : " The Buss of Bridgewater, as she came homeward, to the south-eastward of Frisland, discovered a great island in the latitude of 57 degrees and a half, which was never yet found before, and sailed three days along the coast, the land seeming to be fruitful, full of woods and a champaign country." Later, Thomas Wiars, a passenger in the *Emmanuel*, published an account of the discovery. Buss was duly placed on the maps, but the efforts of reliable searchers failed to locate it again.

It came to be known as " the sunken land of Buss," and was thus noted on charts up to the middle of the nineteenth century. Was Buss submerged ? It seems to be the only acceptable solution of not the least intriguing mystery known to the folklore of the sea.

The discovery of the American mainland by the Norse settlers in Greenland scarcely calls for comment here, unless as another instance of the ancient European folk-memory of land in the Atlantic. But much more valuable testimony to this tradition is to be gleaned from the literature connected with the voyages of the Zeno family of Venice. In 1558 a volume on this subject was printed at Venice which purported to give an account of certain Atlantic islands discovered by Nicolo and Antonio Zeno, two mariners of the city about 1380, and compiled by their descendant, Nicolo Zeno. As given by Major[1] and somewhat abbreviated, the account is as follows :

" Six-and-twenty years ago four fishing boats put out to sea, and, encountering a heavy storm, were driven over the sea in utter helplessness for many days ; . . . the tempest abating, they discovered an island called Estotiland, lying to the westwards above one thousand miles from Frislanda. One of the boats was wrecked, and six men that were in it were taken by the inhabitants . . . into a fair and populous city, where the king of the place sent for many interpreters, but there were none . . . understood the language of the fishermen, except one that spoke Latin, and who had also been cast by chance upon the same island. . . . They . . . remained five years on the island, and learned the language. One of them . . . visited different parts of the island, and reports that it is a very rich country, abounding in all good things. It is a little smaller than Iceland, but more fertile ; in the middle of it is a very high mountain, in which rise four rivers which water the whole country.

" The inhabitants are a very intelligent people, and possess all the arts like ourselves ; and it is to be believed that in time past they have had intercourse with our people, for he said that he saw Latin books in the king's library, which they at this present time do not understand. They

---

[1] *The Voyages of the Brothers Zeno in the Northern Seas in the Fourth Century*, Hakluyt Soc. Publ., 1st Series, Vol. 50.

have their own language and letters . . . all kinds of metals, but especially they abound with gold. Their foreign intercourse is with Greenland, whence they import furs, brimstone and pitch. . . . They have woods of immense extent . . . make their buildings with walls, and there are many towns and villages. They make small boats and sail them, but they have not the loadstone, nor do they know the north by the compass. For this reason these fishermen were held in great esteem . . . the king sent them with twelve small boats . . . southwards to a country which they call Drogio; but in their voyage they had such contrary weather that they were in fear of their lives.

. . . They were taken into the country, and the greater number of them were eaten by savages. . . . But as that fisherman and his remaining companions were able to show them the way of taking fish with nets, their lives were saved. . . . As this man's fame spread . . . there was a neighbouring chief . . . very anxious to have him with him . . . he made war on the chief with whom the fisherman then was, and . . . at length overcame him, and so the fisherman was sent over to him with the rest of his company. During the . . . thirteen years . . . he dwelt in those parts, he says that he was sent . . . to more than five-and-twenty chiefs . . . wandering up and down . . . he became acquainted with almost all those parts. He says . . . it is a very great country, and as it were a new world; the people are . . . rude and uncultivated . . . go naked and suffer cruelly from the cold, nor have they the sense to clothe themselves with the skins of the animals which they take in hunting. They have no kind of metal. They live by hunting, carry lances of wood, sharpened at the point . . . have bows, the strings of which are made of beasts' skins . . . are very fierce, and have deadly fights amongst each other, and eat one another's flesh. . . . The farther you go southwards . . . the more refinement you meet . . . the climate is more temperate . . . they have cities and temples dedicated to their idols, in which they sacrifice men and afterwards eat them.

"His fellow-captives having decided to remain where they were, he bade them farewell, and made his escape through the woods in the direction of Drogio . . . where he spent three years. (One day) some boats had arrived. He . . .

found they had come from Estotiland. (They took him aboard as interpreter.) He afterwards traded in their company . . . became very rich, and, fitting out a vessel, returned to Frislanda."

The elder Zeno heard this story in " Frisland," another " fabulous " Atlantic isle. We observe that the narrator believes that the Estotilanders formerly had intercourse with Europe. Estotiland seems to have been within sailing distance of America, here called Drogio, for the part of the account which deals with Drogio describes a country too closely resembling the east coast of America to present a similarity to any other part of the world. That part of it which deals with human sacrifice seems to point clearly enough to Mexico. In any case, if the account is not a forgery—and good arguments have been advanced for and against its authenticity—it proves that a very definite memory of Atlantic lands was current during the fourteenth century.

That the people of Wales possessed such a tradition is plain from the Welsh legends which cluster round the name of Madoc, Prince of Wales.

This venerable tradition, which has, indeed, given rise to an extensive literature, assures us that on the death of Owen Gwynedd, Prince of North Wales in A.D. 1170, his sons became embroiled in civil strife, and one of them, Madoc, a man experienced in seamanship, disgusted with the unstable condition of the country, resolved to lead a colony to those Western lands of which he had heard his seafaring acquaintances speak. Accordingly, in the year of his father's death, he collected several hundreds of his followers, steered westwards, and eventually established a pioneer colony " in a fertile land." Leaving here one hundred and twenty persons, he returned to Wales, and fitted out a larger expedition of ten ships, with which he once more put to sea, this time passing completely out of human ken.

The evidence in support of this story is that it is mentioned in early Welsh annals, and that numerous travellers have discovered traces of the Welsh language among the lighter-coloured tribes of American Indians, to say nothing of manifold legends among the Indians themselves of a white people coming from afar towards the north-east.

It cannot be said that there is anything wildly improbable about the story. The people of North Wales had been daring seamen for centuries before the reign of Owen Gwynedd, and the vessels of his son, which appear to have sailed from the place now known as Port Madoc, were probably quite as seaworthy and better fitted to stand the buffetings of the Atlantic than those of Columbus. Meredith, a Welsh bard, seems to have celebrated the voyage in some verses composed, according to Hakluyt, in the year 1477, or fifteen years before the Columbian discovery; but the original printed source of the legend is Humphrey Lloyd's *History of Cambria, now called Wales*, which was published at London in 1584. The book was edited and added to by a certain David Powell, and it is in his additions that passages of importance were found. The supposition of Humboldt and others was that Madoc's colony lay near the Gulf of Mexico. Richard Hakluyt in his *Principell Navigatines*, took the story from Powell and connected the discovery with Mexico in his edition of 1589, and with the West Indies in that of 1600. But the *Nieuwe en Onbekende Weereld* of Montanus (Amsterdam, 1671) made the story more familiar. It necessarily entered into the discussions of the learned men who, in the seventeenth century, were busied with the question of the origin of the American races, and among these De Laet and Hornius gave credit to its reality.

The linguistic evidences, however, were not brought into prominence until after one Morgan Jones, a Welsh pastor or missionary, had fallen among the Tuscarora Indians in 1660, and found, as he asserted, that they could understand his Welsh. He wrote an account of his experiences in 1685-6, which was not published until 1740. He is most explicit regarding the ability of his Indian captors to speak the purest Welsh, and states that they perfectly understood those passages of Scripture which he read to them from his Welsh Bible.

It was reported in 1764 that a Welshman of the name of Griffeth had been taken by the Shawnee Indians to visit another tribe who spoke Welsh. An account of his adventures is given in Warren's *Recherches* and Amos Stoddard's *Sketches of Louisiana*. In 1772-3 David Jones, another Welshman, wandered among the tribes west of the Ohio, and in 1774 published at Burlington his *Journal of Two Visits,* in which he indicates the correspondence of words which he found in their tongues with his native Welsh.

The renewed interest in the subject seems to have prompted Southey to the writing of his poem " Madoc," though he refrained from publishing it for some years. If one may judge from his introductory note, Southey held to the historical basis of the narrative. Meanwhile persistent reports were published of the discovery of tribes of Indians who spoke Welsh. In 1816 Henry Kerr printed at Elizabethtown, New Jersey, his *Travels Through the Western Interior of the United States, with some account of a tribe whose customs are similar to those of the ancient Welsh.* Some years later the publication of Catlin's *American Indians* probably gave more conviction than had previously been felt as regards the actuality of the tradition because of his statements of positive linguistic correspondences in the language of the so-called white Mandans of the Missouri, the similarity of their boats to the old Welsh coracles, and other parallels of custom. He believed that Madoc landed in Florida, or perhaps passed up the Mississippi. The opinion of Major in his *Columbus' Letters* (1847) that the Welsh discovery was quite possible, while it was by no means probable is, with little doubt, the view most generally accepted.

If one thing is more clear than another in connection with the legend of Madoc it is that it enshrines a very ancient British tradition concerning the existence of countries in the Atlantic. Did Madoc actually sail ? He cannot have done so unless he had an almost certain knowledge of the existence of territory somewhere in the Atlantic. And if his voyage is the veriest myth, it still shows that his countrymen retained the recollection of such territory.

But if Europeans possessed traditions of an Atlantic continent, did the American races not share that tradition ? We have already seen that they did, but I should like to add in this place one or two extraordinary evidences of historical, as apart from traditional, allusions to the existence of lands and races overseas among the American peoples. When Hernando de Soto, on landing in Peru, first met the Inca Huascar, the latter related an ancient prophecy which his father, Huaina Ccapac, had repeated on his death-bed, that in the reign of the thirteenth Inca white men of surpassing strength and valour would come from their father the Sun and subject the Peruvians to their rule. " I command you," said the dying king, " to yield them homage and obedience, for they will be of a nature superior to ours."[1]

But the most interesting of American legends connected with the discovery is that in which the prophecy of the Maya priest Chilan Balam is described. Father Lizana, a venerable Spanish author, records the prophecy, which he states was very well known throughout Yucatan, as does Villagutierre, who quotes it.

Part of this strange prophecy runs as follows : " At the end of the thirteenth age, when Itza is at the height of its power, as also the city called Tancah, the signal of God will appear on the heights, and the Cross with which the world was enlightened will be manifested. There will be variance of men's will in future times, when this signal shall be brought. . . . Receive your barbarous bearded guests from the east, who bring the signal of God, who comes to us in mercy and pity. The time of our life is coming. . . ."

The story of Princess Papantzin, sister of Montezuma the Emperor of Mexico, who had a strange vision of white men coming from across the sea, also seems to show that a powerful tradition respecting. white races which had formerly visited the American continent existed so late as the sixteenth century. The royal lady's vision so strongly affected her imperial brother that he refused to consider the possibility of opposing the Spaniards, designating them " Sons of Quetzalcoatl," whom he believed to be of divine or superior origin, and who, he thought, were the servants of the god, returning according to his long-standing promise. Surely these promises and visions are eloquent of the memory of a civilizing race which formerly landed on American shores, from whom the native peoples had imbibed their culture and whose former presence was regarded not as legendary but historical.

---

[1] Garcilasso el Inca de la Vega, *Hist. des Incas*, lib. ix, cap. 15.

CHAPTER XI

THE ANALOGY OF LEMURIA

A CONSIDERATION of the allied problem of the sunken continent of Lemuria in the Pacific area greatly illuminates the problems attending the theory of Atlantis, for it has been proved almost beyond the possibility of doubt that many presently existing populations of the Pacific Islands once occupied land areas now submerged, it has been proved that Pacific islands have disappeared within living memory, and that land-masses of comparatively large area have been drowned beneath Pacific waters within the last few centuries. Moreover, a mass of tradition far too widespread to be void of significance, much too clamorous and important to be dismissed by the wave of a conservative hand, renders it abundantly clear that the peoples of the Pacific possess the irrefragable historical memory of not one but several masses of sunken land which were probably the decaying remnants of one or more far-flung continents.

The theory of a former mid-Atlantic continent has at least as many opponents as it can boast supporters. But, paradoxically enough, the belief that a great land-mass once occupied the basin of the Pacific is accepted by the majority of modern geologists, even the most conservative agreeing that from the Primary to the Secondary geological period an immense continent, ringed round with an ocean which communicated with the Arctic, occupied the greater part of the present Pacific area. At the end of the Primary Period this ocean flowed over what is now the region of the Andes and the present Rocky Mountains on the east, and above New Zealand, Melanesia and Papuasia, the Phillipines and Japan on the west. By the end of the Secondary Period the Pacific continent had begun to founder, and the west coast of South America to rise correspondingly. So much is generally conceded. It is only regarding the approximate period of the ultimate disappearance of the last vestiges of this continent that debate arises, and if it arises at all it is because the data in favour of the quite recent existence of numerous large island-groups in the Pacific has only recently been collected and published.

The hypothesis of a great Pacific continent was first

mooted by Dr. Augustus Gould in 1854 in a striking paper,
" Remarks on Mollusks and Shells," published in *The
Edinburgh New Philosophical Journal.* Charles Darwin in
his *Journal of Researches* (1889) demonstrated that the
formation of coral reefs and atolls demanded a long-
continued subsidence of the Pacific region, and acting on
his suggestion, Professors Sollas and David undertook the
boring of the atoll of Funafuti to a depth of 1114 feet,
where cores were obtained which showed that the whole
mass of rock was composed of pure coral. As the organisms
which form coral reefs cannot live at a depth of more than
150 feet, it was manifest that the ocean floor must slowly
and continuously have subsided.

In 1884 Hutton, in his *Origin of Flora and Fauna of New
Zealand,* advanced the theory that New Zealand, Eastern
Australia and India formed one biological region in the
Secondary Period, and that in Lower Cretaceous times a
large Pacific continent extended from Lower Guinea to
Chile. Later on, he thought, New Zealand became
separated and this continent broke up.

Von Ihering believed the Pacific land-mass to have
gradually subsided during the Secondary Period, and
Dr. Pilsbry was of opinion that it was finally separated
from other lands as early as the middle of that period,
and that the northern portion became disconnected when
the remainder was still joined to the mainland. A careful
review of some of the lesser fauna, especially of ants and
lizards, led Professor Baur to formulate the theory of a
former Indo-Pacific continent extending from Malaysia to
the west coast of America. He looked upon the Pacific
islands as the last remnants of this continent, which still
existed, he thought, until the commencement of the
Miocene Period in Tertiary times.

Mr. Speight in his *Petrological Notes from the Kermadec
Islands* presents geological evidence of the former extension of continental conditions over a large area of the mid-
Pacific region. Many volcanic islands, he remarks, now
classified as oceanic, will ultimately have to be regarded
as having been built up out of the remnants of a continental area. He believes that a continent covered the
greater part of the Pacific Ocean in Primary and early
Secondary times, and that a subsidence occurred during

later Secondary and Tertiary times with more recent local elevations.

The well-known parallelism of the several groups of the Pacific islands has been advanced as an argument in favour of a formerly existing Pacific continent. It seems possible to explain this " lay of the land " by the supposition that these islands are the remains of a series of mountain-chains, as has been suggested by Herr T. Arldt.

Professor Francis Scharff in his *Origin of Life in America* remarks : " If a Pacific continent existed, and I quite concur with those who are of that opinion, it must have largely subsided before the Tertiary era. It seems to me as if the central part of it had broken down gradually, the margins slowly following suit, both on the eastern and western Pacific, only leaving here and there a few remnants which either remain as isolated pillars far out in the ocean or have become joined to more recent land-masses. I imagine that the latest pre-Pliocene land connection between North America and Asia was not the Pacific continent but merely its margin, which persisted probably until Oligocene or Miocene times. . . . I suggest that in Tertiary times a belt of land, possibly representing the margin of the more ancient Pacific continent, extended from the south-west coast to North America in a great curve to Japan and further south."

There is, however, Professor Scharff admits, an extraordinary amount of evidence that an ancient land occupied that portion of the Pacific contiguous to the west coast of Guatemala. The present Central America is, he thinks, " partly formed of the remnants of that land having eventually become moulded together by geologically recent volcanic deposits." Mr. O. H. Hershey is of opinion that this ancient land lay mainly south of the present isthmus of Panama, and that it was a land-mass of considerable extent is indicated by the heavy beds of conglomerate formed from it.

There seems to be good reason for the inference that this Pacific land persisted until comparatively recent geological times. Agassiz found that not a single station between Acapulco on the west coast of Mexico and the Galapagos Islands could be characterised as strictly oceanic. The trawl brought up a sticky mud containing logs of wood, branches, twigs and decayed vegetable matter.

Dr. Burckhardt argued from the enormously thick deposits of porphyrite conglomerates in Western Chile that these were laid down on the ancient shore-line of a vast western land-mass of which the existing coast cordillera of Chile is the last remnant. Says Scharff, dealing with Burckhardt's theory : " He advocates, in fact, nothing short of what we might call a Pacific continent which lay mainly to the westward of Chile. That land formerly extended in that direction I have endeavoured to demonstrate from purely faunistic evidence, but I believe that it was part of a great circum-Pacific belt of land which stretched mainly northward, communicating from time to time with Central America and the Antilles, and also with Mexico and Western California, and then eventually bending across to Eastern Asia in a great loop and thus joining New Guinea, Australia and New Zealand."

A more recent protagonist of the theory of a great Pacific continent from the fragments of which Polynesian civilisation emerged is Professor J. Macmillan Brown of Christchurch, New Zealand, who, in his recent remarkable work, *The Riddle of the Pacific,* has reviewed the whole subject with impartiality and a marked capacity for dealing with a problem of such complexity in a simple manner. In a passage which will certainly become memorable in the annals of the controversy which has raged so long around the subject of sunken land-areas, he says : " Whether we assume a continental area in the central region of the Pacific or not, there must have been enormously more land than there is now, if not some land connection between the Hawaiian Archipelago and the south-west of Polynesia ; for the American scientists, working from the former, find a close affinity between its flora and fauna and those of the latter, whilst there is no evidence of connection with the American continent. In the flora, for example, the only great genera of the south-west that are absent in the north-east are the aroids, ficoids and pines. The affinity of the land-shells is even more convincing. But the north and south connection was the first to disappear, leaving traces in scattered coral islands like Washington, Fanning, Christmas, Malden, Manihiki. The trend of the ancient high land was from north-west to south-east. And as the archipelagoes from New Zealand through Melanesia, Papuasia, Indonesia, the Philippines and Japan rose, Micronesia and Southern Polynesia sank ; and from the Mariannes down to Mangareva and Easter Island there are more coral islands than in any other region of the world. . . . In the Pacific Ocean, at least, wherever there is a coral island there has been subsidence, even if followed by elevation. And it is to be granted that along with subsidence in the coral arcs of the Pacific there is sporadic elevation. For the volcanic activity that raised the high land primevally becomes not suddenly but slowly quiescent. In some coral groups there are volcanic islands, as the Tongan, Samoan, Society and Marquesan groups ; and raised coral islands like Niue and Rimatara are not infrequent. In fact there is clear evidence of alternate subsidences and elevations ; the phosphate islands, Makatea in the northwest of the Paumotus and Ocean Island and Nauru in the west of the Gilberts, have gone down to leach out the nitrates of their blanket of bird manure and come up to have a new blanket several times. And away in the southeast of the Pacific the rise of the two Cordilleras of the Andes along the coast of South America must have had full compensation in subsidence ; and this is apparent in the long stretch of the Paumotus and the almost islandless seas to the south of them. Nor has this rise of the South American coast ceased. The great earthquakes and tidal waves that have devastated portions of it in historical times make it patent, and the elevation of the coast is measurable within brief periods."

But we have more than mere geological surmise to go upon in discussing the possibility of the existence of very considerable land-areas in the Pacific only a few centuries ago and which must have undergone submergence. The logs of the navigators of the seventeenth century contain more than one allusion to Pacific land-masses of large extent now no longer visible. In his *Description of the Isthmus of Darien*, published at London in 1688, Wafer describes how when sailing in the ship *The Bachelor's Delight* in lat. 27° 20' south, " to the westward, about twelve leagues by judgment, we saw a range of high land which we took to be islands. . . . This land seemed to reach about fourteen or fifteen leagues in a range, and there came thence great flocks of fowls." *The Bachelor's Delight* was commanded by John Davis, a Dutchman in spite of his English name, and had just experienced a severe submarine shock which proved to be the earthquake of Callao of 1687.

Thirty-five years later the Dutch Admiral Ruggewein sailed along the same latitude in search of " Davis Land," but could not locate it or discover any signs of it. But to compensate for his disappointment he discovered Easter Island on Easter Day. In 1771 Gonzalez, a Spanish navigator, likewise sailed in search of Davis Land, and, like his predecessor, came upon Easter Island. This island resembles not at all the land which Davis and Wafer saw, as Beechy, who visited the island in 1825, declares, so that it is positively certain that an island or archipelago of considerable extent foundered in this area of the Pacific at some time between 1687 and 1722.

But there is evidence forthcoming long before the date of Davis's discovery that land had vanished in this region. Juan Fernandez in 1576 went out of his course when sailing between Callao and Valparaiso, and encountered what he believed to be the coast of that great southern continent which so many of the seamen of his day dreamed of. He saw " the mouths of very large rivers . . . and people so white and so well clad and in everything different from those of Chile and Peru " that he was amazed. His ship was small and ill-found, and he resolved to return, meanwhile keeping what he had seen secret. But he died without fulfilling his purpose. As late as 1909 the ship *Guinevere* reported a reef in about 95 long. east and 35 lat. south, which may be the remains of the land Fernandez saw.

There are several well-authenticated instances of the entire submergence of islands in the Pacific during last century. In 1836 the island of Tuanaki, to the south of the Cook group, disappeared. Two natives of the Mangaian group had landed there and remained for some time, and reported to the missionaries at Mangaia that its people were anxious to embrace Christianity. The missionary schooner was dispatched to the island under the guidance of these native sailors, " but it never found the island, and no one has seen it since, although up till recently there was at least one native living in Rarotonga who had lived in it and one who had visited it. Had the two Mangaians not landed on it and reported it to the missionaries, would anyone ever have known of the submergence of it and its people ? There might have been a vague rumour, easily believed and easily discounted, and that would have been all the record," remarks Professor Brown.

The traditions of Easter Island maintain that it was once the hub or centre of a large, scattered archipelago. The culture-hero Hotu Matua was forced to land on its shores, says legend, because of the submergence of his own island, Marae Ronga, to the west, where "the sea came up and drowned all the people." There are numerous reefs round Sala-y-Gomez, a rocky islet about three hundred miles east of Easter Island, and the natives tell how this islet was once a large archipelago, of which a certain Makemake was the prince. When Hotu Matua came to his death-day he ascended a volcano in Easter Island and looked out towards the west, calling to the spirits who hovered over his submerged home. The legends of Easter Island are full of reminiscences of other neighbouring islands now drowned beneath the surface of the Pacific. The immense dry-stone monuments of Easter Island, says Professor Brown, could not have been raised by an insular people, but must have taxed the capacity of a great contiguous archipelagic empire, maintaining thousands of people of Polynesian stock.

But other mysterious cyclopean ruins besides those of Easter Island are to be encountered in the widely scattered archipelagoes of the Pacific, and equally important are the theories of submergence associated with them. By far the most important and perplexing of these sites is that at Ponape in the Caroline Islands, lying between the equator and the eleventh north parallel, some two thousand three hundred miles from the coast of Japan. The deserted city of Metalanim, the ruins of which cover eleven square miles, stands on the south-eastern shore of Ponape. The site is covered by massive walls, stupendous earthworks and great temples, intersected by miles of artificial waterways, from which circumstance it has received the name of "The Venice of the Pacific."

The entire island of Ponape is littered with huge basaltic

blocks which must have been brought by raft from a distance of thirty miles, and from similar blocks have been built stupendous walls of the harbour and the embankments of the winding canals, many of which are from 80 to 100 feet in breadth. The outer cincture which surrounds the city is partially submerged, and this has given rise to the idea that the land on which Metalanim was built has subsided in later times. It is clear that the waterways were constructed to enable rafts laden with stone to be brought close up to the artificial islands on which the larger buildings were raised.

The city of Metalanim was enclosed on one side by the land and on its maritime side by three extensive breakwaters of basalt, the whole occupying an almost rectangular area. At the north-west corner a sea-gate gave entrance to vessels and rafts of considerable dimensions, and this was carefully guarded by a large breakwater consisting of immense courses of the basalt characteristic of the site. The water front to the east is faced by a terrace built of massive blocks about 7 feet in width, above which frowns the vast retaining wall of the enclosure of Nan Tanach, " The Place of Lofty Walls." A colossal staircase leads to a courtyard littered with the fragments of fallen pillars which encircle a second terraced enclosure with a projecting frieze or cornice. Here lies the great central vault or " treasure-chamber " of a legendary dynasty known to local tradition as the Chanteleur, or " Kings of the Sun."

The reader who has perused Plato's account of Atlantis will not fail to remark upon the likeness between the general plan of Metalanim and the city of Atlas. Both were intersected with canals, both had great sea-gates and sea-walls, and two or three rows of walls encircling the city proper. Had Atlantean and Lemurian civilisation and culture anything in common ? A future comparative study of the conditions obtaining in both may cast more light on this phase of the subject, to which I hope to return at another time.

Nan Tanach, the hub of the city, seems to have been the nucleus whence the numerous canals radiated throughout the whole ghostly length of the place. It is surmised that the great blocks of which it is built were put in position by means of an inclined plane—a slope of tree-trunks, greased with coconut oil. The process of hoisting may have been assisted by the use of ropes made of the green hibiscus bark and levers of hardwood.

It is obvious that the Caroline Islands at the period of the occupation of this site must have supported a very much larger population than they do at the present time. At a conservative estimate, tens of thousands of labourers must have been engaged in the work of building-construction at Metalanim. The island at its best could never have supported more than twenty thousand people, and of these not more than one-fifth would be able-bodied men, therefore it is only reasonable to suppose that labour must have been recruited from outside areas. Professor Macmillan Brown suggests as a solution to this difficulty that the Caroline archipelago is the remains of a vast island-empire, the greater part of which has subsided beneath the waves of the Pacific centuries ago. Yet within a radius of fifteen hundred miles from this as a centre there are not more than fifty thousand people to-day.

A thousand miles to the west of Ponape Professor Brown found on the little coral island of Oleai, with six hundred inhabitants, a written script still in use, quite unlike any in the world. It is still used by the chief of the island, and was formerly employed on Faraulep, an islet about one hundred miles to the north-east. On the east coast of the island of Yap there is a village called Gatsepar, the chief of which still levies tribute annually on islands hundreds of miles away. When Professor Brown asked the natives who brought the tribute why they continued to do so, they replied that if they neglected this duty the chief of Gatsepar would shake their island with his earthquakes and the sea with his tempests. This would seem to imply, thinks Professor Brown, that the chief's ancestors built " an empire to the east of Yap, and when some intermediate islands had gone down, the others continued still to look to the ruler in the west as the holder of all power, natural and supernatural."

Is there any evidence of similar submersion of organised archipelagoes farther east ? Polynesia covers a greater space than most of the larger empires of the world have covered, and is occupied by a people more homogeneous in physique, culture and language than the people of any one of the great empires. In handicraft, social and political organisation and religious belief they exhibit the remains of a very high type of civilisation, and it is obvious that they have been segregated from other races for a space of time so prolonged that an indelible and easily distinguishable mark has been set upon them. "We can scarcely avoid the conclusion," says Professor Brown, "that they have lived unitedly under one government and under one social system for a long period ; and that the slow submergence of their fatherland has driven them off, migration after migration, to seek other lands to dwell upon, each marked by some new habit into which they were driven by the gradual narrowing of their cultivable area. . . . All the indications point to an empire in the east Central Pacific having gone down."

And if such a phenomenon occurred in the Pacific area, why not in the Atlantic also ? Do not all the indications point to the former existence of an empire in the Atlantic region, and to the subsequent diffusion of its culture ? In my view the light which Professor Macmillan Brown has cast upon the problem of the Pacific throws also not a few vivid gleams upon the problem of Atlantis, and it now remains by closer study to so collate the parallel circumstances of the two problems that the lessons of Pacific archæology may be adequately applied to the Atlantean question.

CHAPTER XII

THE SARGASSO SEA

THE *Arcturus* expedition, which is at present investigating the mysterious Sargasso Sea, in the Atlantic, has at the time of writing sent a wireless message to the New York press reporting the discovery of glass, volcanic rock and sponge deposits from the bed of the Sargasso. The chief purpose of the expedition, which has been conveyed to the weed-covered wastes of the Sargasso in the converted yacht *Arcturus*, is to explore this little-known region of the Atlantic, to determine whether the weed of which it is composed is blown out from the land or propagates itself, and to photograph the strange forms of life which infest the area.

The Sargasso Sea is traditionally associated with the sunken continent of Atlantis. Many writers have asserted their belief that in its area the site of Plato's submerged island is to be found, and extraordinary reports have for years been in circulation regarding the imprisonment in its enormous fields of floating weed of flotillas of sea-going vessels ancient and modern, from the triremes of Tyre to the modern steamship. This latter notion is, of course, a gross exaggeration, arising out of the persistent traditions of centuries. There is, however, good ground for the opinion that if the weed of the Sargasso does not constitute the last visible remnant of Atlantis that its site is probably identical with that of the lost island-continent.

Perhaps the most surprising thing about the Sargasso is that so much dubiety should exist concerning its actual character in an age when almost every square mile of the earth's surface has been traversed and mapped out by travellers and navigators. For it is one of the permanent and conspicuous features of the earth's surface, a floating continent of weed, shifting its borders with the seasons, although in some parts it is constant in its characteristics. A writer in the *Encyclopædia Britannica* describes it as nearly equal to Europe in area, but this statement is certainly incorrect. Otto Krümmel in his *Die Nordatlantische Sargassosee*[1] suggests that the name should be applied to the area only which is limited by the occurrence of 5 per cent of weed. This area is 4,500,000 kilometres

[1] Pethermann's " Mitt.," Vol. 37, pp. 129–41, 1891,

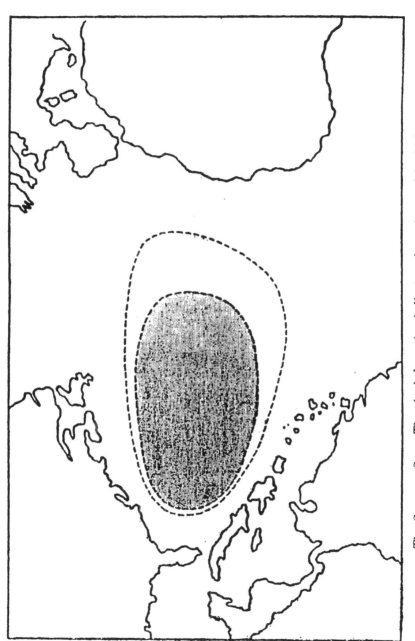

The Sargasso Sea. The shaded portion indicates where the weed is thickest.

square, or somewhat less than half the continent of Europe,
and would embrace a tract extending from the 30th
parallel of longitude to the Antilles, and from the 40th
to the 20th parallel of latitude. Schott estimates the extent of the natural region of the Sargasso Sea at 8,635,000
square kilometres, and this estimate is based not only on
the occurrence of gulf weed, but also on the prevailing
absence of currents and on the relatively high temperature
of the water in all depths.

Regarding the weed which characterises this part of the
Atlantic, Sir John Murray says :

" The famous Gulf Weed characteristic of the Sargasso
Sea in the North Atlantic belongs to the brown algæ.
It is named *Sargassum bacciferum*, and is easily recognised
by its small berry-like bladders. . . . It is supposed that
the older patches gradually lose their power of floating
and perish by sinking in deep water. . . . The floating
masses of Gulf Weed are believed to be continually
replenished by additional supplies torn from the coast by
waves and carried by currents until they accumulate in
the great Atlantic whirl which surrounds the Sargasso
Sea. They become covered with white patches of polyzoa
and serpulæ, and quite a large number of other animals
(small fishes, crabs, prawns, molluscs, etc.) live on these
masses of weed in the Sargasso Sea, all exhibiting remarkable adaptive colouring, although none of them belong
properly to the open ocean."

Lieut. J. C. Soley of the U.S. Navy in his *Circulation of
the North Atlantic* states that the south-east branch of the
Gulf Stream " runs in the direction of the Azores, where
it is deflected by the cold, upwelling stream from the
north, and runs into the centre of the Atlantic Basin,
where it is lost in the dead waters of the Sargasso Sea."
Commenting on this, the U.S. Hydrographic Office
observes : " Through the dynamical forces arising from
the earth's rotation which cause moving masses in the
northern hemisphere to be deflected toward the right-hand
side of their path, the algæ that are borne by the Gulf
Stream from the tropical seas find their way towards the
inner edge of the circulatory drift which moves in a clock-
wise direction around the central part of the North Atlantic
Ocean. In this central part the flow of the surface waters

is not steady in any direction, and hence the floating sea-weed tends to accumulate there. This accumulation is perhaps most observable in the triangular region marked out by the Azores, the Canaries and the Cape Verde Islands, but much seaweed is also found to the westward of the middle part of this region in an elongated area extending to the 70th meridian.

" The abundance of seaweed in the Sargasso Sea fluctuates much with the variation of the agencies which account for its presence, but this office does not possess any authentic records to show that it has ever materially impeded vessels."

With reference to this passage Mr. W. H. Babcock remarks in his *Legendary Islands of the Atlantic*:

" Perhaps these statements are influenced by present or recent conditions. It is obvious that giant rope-like seaweeds in masses would more than materially impede the action of the galley oars, which were the main reliance in time of calm of the ancient and medieval navigators. Also it is hardly to be believed that small sailing vessels could freely drive through them with an ordinary wind. If the weeds were so unobstructive, why all these complaints and warnings out of remote centuries ? In the days of powerful steamships, and when the skippers of sailing vessels have learned what area of sea it is best to avoid, there may well be a lack of formal reports of impediment ; but it certainly looks as though there were some basis for the long-established ill repute of the Sargasso Sea."

As Mr. Babcock states, there is a large body of testimony that in ancient times the Atlantic was unnavigable, and that the Sargasso Sea formerly occupied a much larger area. The first hint of this is to be found in Plato's *Critias*, which embodies the original account of the sunken continent of Atlantis beneath the waves. Since the founding of Atlantis, says Plato, " the sea in these quarters has become unnavigable ; vessels cannot pass there because of the sands which extend over the buried isle." In this passage the Greek philosopher is not alluding to past but present conditions, conditions which any of his contemporaries could verify for themselves by applying to any of the numerous Greek or Phœnician mariners who had

experience of those waters. "It must be evident," says
Mr. Babcock, "that Plato would not have written thus
unless he relied on the established general repute of that
part of the ocean for difficulty of navigation."

But Plato's account is buttressed by those of other
writers of antiquity. Scylax of Caryanda, who wrote prior
to the time of Alexander the Great, and was approximately
a contemporary of Plato, states in his *Periplus* that Cerne,
an island on the African Atlantic coast, "is twelve days
coasting beyond the Pillars of Hercules, where the parts
are no longer navigable because of shoals, of mud and of
seaweed. . . . The seaweed has the width of a palm, and
is sharp towards the points so as to prick."

When Himilco parted from Hanno in the course of their
memorable dual voyage from Carthage in quest of lands
unknown about 500 B.C., he encountered, according to the
poet Festus Avienus, "weeds, shallows, calms and dangers"
in the Atlantic. Avienus wrote about the fourth century
A.D., but professes to repeat Himilco's account. He says :
" No breeze drives the ship forward, so dead is the sluggish
wind of this idle sea. He (Himilco) also adds that there is
much seaweed among the waves, and that it often holds
the ship back like bushes. Nevertheless he says that the
sea has no great depth, and that the surface of the earth
is barely covered by a little water. The monsters of the
sea move continually hither and thither, and the wild
beasts swim among the sluggish and slowly creeping ships."
Avienus also says elsewhere : " Farther to the west from
these Pillars there is boundless sea. Himilco relates that
. . . none has sailed ships over these waters, because
propelling winds are lacking . . . likewise because darkness screens the light of day with a sort of clothing, and
because a fog always conceals the sea."

Aristotle, too, says in his *Meteorologica* that the sea
beyond the Pillars of Hercules was muddy and shallow and
almost unstirred by the winds. Aristotle was at one time
a pupil of Plato, and this would seem to afford good proof
that the latter's statement was founded on the best available information, and was probably acquired from
Phœnician or Greek seamen.

But we have other than classical evidence for the unnavigable character of the Atlantic, evidence dating from

a considerably later period. Edrisi, the Arabic writer, says that the Magrurin, certain Moorish sailors of Lisbon who set sail thence in quest of an Atlantic island at some undefined period between the eighth and twelfth centuries, encountered an impassable tract of ocean, and were forced to alter their course, apparently reaching one of the Canaries. The Pizagani map of 1367, too, has a rubric containing a solemn protest against attempting to sail the unnavigable ocean tract beyond the Azores, in the neighbourhood of which the Sargasso Sea begins.

Maury in his *Physical Geography of the Sea* says : " Midway the Atlantic, in the triangular space between the Azores, Canaries and the Cape de Verd Islands, is the Sargasso Sea. Covering an area equal in extent to the Mississippi Valley, it is so thickly matted over with Gulf Weeds (*Fucus natans*) that the speed of vessels passing through it is often much retarded. When the companions of Columbus saw it they thought it marked the limits of navigation, and became alarmed. To the eye, at a little distance, it seems substantial enough to walk upon. Patches of the weed are always to be seen floating along the outer edge of the Gulf Stream. Now, if bits of cork, or chaff, or any floating substance be put in a basin and a circular motion be given to the water, all the light substances will be found crowding together near the centre of the pool where there is the least motion. Just such a basin is the Atlantic Ocean to the Gulf Stream ; and the Sargasso Sea is the centre of the whirl. Columbus first found this weedy sea in his voyage of discovery ; there it has remained to this day, moving up and down, and changing its position like the calms of Cancer according to the seasons, the storms and the winds. Exact observations as to its limits and their range, extending back for fifty years, assure us that its mean position has not been altered since that time."

The notion that the Sargasso weed is a collection of the floating detritus of the Atlantic is by no means justified by the related facts. In the first place Sir John Murray admits that the shell-fish and other animals which live amongst the weed " all exhibit adaptive colouring, although none of them belong properly to the open ocean." Adaptive colouring, as in the Arctic hare and ptarmigan, requires countless centuries for its development, and is an especial trait evolved out of long-continued adaptation to local conditions. This fact alone, coupled with the classical evidence, would seem to show that the Sargasso weed must have persisted for thousands of years. Again, it is most improbable that these forms of coastal life could have reached the Sargasso by an open ocean route. Is it not more reasonable to infer that they are the survivors of forms which once occupied a coast-line, now submerged, in the same locality where they now appear ?

Weed of the same species as is found in the Sargasso occurs in the Pacific Ocean, west of California, which is undoubtedly another area where land was formerly submerged. But the main point is that this Sargasso accumulation undoubtedly occupies part of the same area as did the now sunken mass of Atlantis. The argument in favour of the former existence of Atlantis is, however, not dependent upon the identification of these sites.

" Another remarkable feature of the North Atlantic is the series of submerged cones or oceanic shoals made known off the north-west coast of Africa between the Canary Islands and the Spanish peninsula," says Sir John Murray. But, important as these seem to be to an elucidation of the Atlantean theory in the opinion of Mr. W. H. Babcock, I believe the great bank mapped out by the several expeditions which undertook the survey of the Atlantic towards the latter part of last century in the *Hydra, Porcupine, Challenger* and *Dolphin* to be more important still. This bank commences at a point south of the coast of Ireland, is traversed by the 53rd parallel, and stretches in a direction which embraces the Azores toward the African coast. The general level of this great ridge or plateau is some 9000 feet above that of the bed of the Atlantic. Other immense banks stretch from Iceland almost to the South American coast, where they adjoin the old sunken land of Antillia. It is precisely above the area where the great sunken plateaus converge, that is between the 40th and 60th parallels of longitude and the 20th and 40th parallels of latitude, that the Sargasso weed is thickest.

Thus reliable evidence exists for the assumption that the area of the Sargasso Sea coincides with that of sunken

Atlantis. A much greater amount of proof that the weed of which it is composed is in some manner connected with the detritus of the sunken continent is certainly desirable. The accounts of Plato and others suggest that the weed is the vegetable flotsam of Atlantis. Not only does the coincidence of areas between the Sargasso and the site of Atlantis assist such a hypothesis. The antiquity of the classical allusions to the Sargasso accumulation and the obviously wider area it occupied in ancient times appear to strengthen it. But undoubtedly further research into the biological character of the Sargasso algæ and its incidence elsewhere is essential before anything approaching a final decision as to its connection with Atlantis can be arrived at.

CHAPTER XIII

ATLANTIS IN AMERICA

WITH the proof of the dissemination of Atlantean civilisation in America furnished by the foregoing chapters it may not be regarded as an extravagance of nomenclature if I allude to the wonderful culture of the Maya as constituting " Atlantis in America."

I have concluded that the Maya civilisation was an Atlantean offshoot because I do not see from what other part of the world it could have emanated. That it did not germinate of itself on American soil is clear from the fact that its roots are not to be found there. Its traditions are eloquent of its eastern and Atlantic origin. To argue that it was conveyed in its completeness and entirety from Asia across more than five thousand miles of ocean at a period some two centuries before the Christian era is to speak à l'amateur. I agree, then, with Professor J. Macmillan Brown that if you cannot find a neighbouring locus for the cultural origins of an isolated people, that there is nothing unreasonable in seeking for it in a submerged area. The notions regarding the exclusively American or Asiatic origin of the Maya culture are demonstrably illogical : that concerning its Atlantean-Antillian origin is more in consonance with proven facts, and is reinforced by proof of cultural connection with lands which shared equally with America in the benefits of Atlantean civilisation.

I believe that the Maya, on the submergence of their original home in Antillia, temporarily occupied some of the more westerly of the West Indian Islands, the Greater Antilles, from which they withdrew to the Central American mainland at some time about 200 B.C.[1] That they were more or less prone to sudden migratory impulses we know from the fact that later they quitted Guatemala for Yucatan in the sixth century of our era. Probably they found the rude inhabitants of the Greater Antilles but little amenable to the influences of civilisation, and resolved to push onward to the isthmian regions beyond. More probably still, they were harassed by the barbarous Carib. There remains also the likelihood that they were, through

---

[1] I believe the Lesser Antilles to be the last westerly fragment of the Antillian land-mass. The Maya would naturally vacate or pass these and settle in the more stable western islands.

sad experience, dubious of the stability of the insular
regions they occupied, or, again, as on the occasion of their
migration to Yucatan, they may have believed themselves
to be called to another territory by the divine behest of
their national gods.

Contemporaneously with their arrival in America, we
find this strange and interesting people utilising with a
certainty and directness eloquent of age-long experience
a system of astrological and astronomical science on a
much higher plane than was known to the nations of
antiquity in the Old World. They computed time in
æons of centuries by means of a system scarcely credible
except by students who have devoted themselves to its
diligent study. As a check upon their calculations, they
used the recurring periods of the planet Venus with a
nicety of mathematical accuracy which fixed the reappear-
ance of that luminary within a few hours of its actual
visibility. The dates on their very earliest known monuments display the use of the " Venus periods," as they
have come to be known to Americanists. A similar but
much less elaborate system of computation by the aid of
this planet was known in Peru, but not in Asia, either
anciently or in times contemporary with the period of
Maya civilisation in its heyday.

Where, then, originated this most accurate and advanced
astronomical science, which, all those who have examined
it are at one in saying, was greatly superior to that in use
among the Spanish discoverers and conquerors of the
Maya ? To say that it was developed upon American soil
is equally fatuous with the declaration that it was brought
from Asia, where there are no signs of its existence. The
planet Venus was, in Mexico, inseparably connected with
the witch-cult. It was known in that country as Itzlacoliuhqui, "the star that proceeds in a reverse course with
its eyes bandaged." It was identified with Cinteotl, the
son of the witch-queen Tlazolteotl. Its identification with
the Atlantis culture-complex as demonstrated in these
pages is therefore complete, especially when we find it
represented in the Codex Borgia and elsewhere as a mummy
bandaged and swathed for burial. It was during the aspects
of Venus, which were regarded as astrologically unfavour-
able, that the dead witch-women, the Ciuateteô, came down

to wreak their spite on the living. The planet Venus affords yet another link between the witch-cult and mummy phases of the peculiar Atlantean culture-complex. In some places, too, it is represented in the form of Itzlacoliuhqui as the thunder-stone, the witch's bolt or arrow. The thunder-stone is in many American and West European localities carefully wrapped in swathings of cloth or hide, precisely as is the mummy.

Now this thunder-stone is universally feared by primitive peoples as the source of all tempests, earthquakes and

Itzlacoliuhqui, the planet Venus, showing bandaged eyes.

volcanic phenomena. It was the bolt of Vulcan, the dreaded elf-arrow of Scotland, the tempest-raising Neevougi of the Atlantic Irish isles, the weapon of the Phœnician Cabiri and the Mexican Tezcatlipoca alike. In Europe it seems to have been identified with the volcanic scoriæ belched from the erupting jaws of Mount Etna. For this and other reasons, therefore, I believe the supernatural ideas associated with it to have originated in some region prone to seismic activity. In any case it connects and links up the witch and mummy cults with the notion of seismic instability. In the western Irish isle of Fladdahuan if you unwound its many linen bandages you precipitated a tempest. In Mexico the god Hurakan, "the hurricane," was the Central American equivalent of the stone god Itzlacoliuhqui, the knife of sacrifice wrapped in mummy bandages, the god of the planet Venus. Like Vulcan, too, as his myth records, he was lamed through being cast from heaven, so that he had obviously a volcanic significance like the god of Etna.

Behind such a tangle of similarities there must surely be some common original conception. It seems to me that the idea of the thunder-stone arose out of the conception that it was the germ, essence, or principle of the tempest, the thing that caused violent conditions in nature, winds or earthquakes, or eruptions. As we shall see, it was the implement with which the gods shaped the earth and was therefore of itself a magical tool, which on occasion might automatically undertake the functions of earth-heaping or mountain-carving with disastrous results. But if you wrapped it up in bandages, that is, made a mummy of it, it was temporarily dead, and powerless for evil. If you unwound its wrappings you let loose its " soul," with all its potentialities for destruction. If you were a witch you could with impunity handle this magical implement, full of a divine virtue from its contact with the creating god. At least the fishermen of Ireland believed that you could. It is less than fifty years ago that a supernatural being known as Brounger, who was " a flint and the son of a flint," was credited by the fishermen of Granton, a fishing village near Edinburgh, with strange powers. The local tradition goes that they paid him tribute of soles and flounders, and the saying " Brounger's in your head-sheets " was tantamount to calling down a storm upon the boat of a rival. Brounger, the flint, was, indeed, a god of the storm.

As evidently bearing a relationship to this hypothesis, mention may be made of the curious three-pointed stones which are found in some parts of the Antilles. The geographical distribution of these is confined to Porto Rico and the adjacent eastern end of Santo Domingo, that is, to that part of the Antilles which must either have formed a portion of the submerged Antillia or have been nearest to it. These stones are usually carved in the shape of a mountain beneath which the head and legs of a buried recumbent figure is to be seen. Professor Mason hints

that they may be connected with the volcanic history of
the island. "The Antilles," he writes, "are all of volcanic
origin, as the material of our stone implements plainly
shows. I am indebted to Professor S. F. Baird for the
suggestion that, from the sea, the island of Porto Rico
rises in an abrupt and symmetrical manner, highly suggestive of the mound in the mammiform stones, so that with
the aid of a little imagination we may see in these objects
the genius of Porto Rico in the figure of a man, a parrot,
an alligator, an albatross, or some other animal precious
to these regions where larger animals are not abundant,
supporting the island on its back."

Elsewhere, dealing with the legend of Typhœus, slain
by Jupiter and buried under Mount Etna, he remarks :
"A similar myth may have been devised in various places
to account for volcanic or mountainous phenomena."

According to Agustin Navarette, Dr. Calixto Romero
Cantero recognised in these three-pointed figures the genius
of evil weighed down by the god Borinquen, represented
by the mountain Lucuo or Luquillo, and symbolised by
the conoid prominence on the stones. Navarette believes
these stones to be cosmo-theogonic symbols conforming
perfectly to a tradition given by Buret de Longchamps.
"The cone," he says, "is chaos, from which in the form
of sunken rocks arose Taraxtaihetomos, the original
creator, perfectly defined, represented by the head, and
Tepapa, the inert, unformed matter, represented by the
posterior part. In a word this figure is a zemi, the unique
Indo-Borinqueno idol, in which is symbolised the creator
and inert matter on two sides of chaos, which extends over
the firmament."[1]

This explanation errs, perhaps, too much on the side of
symbolism. Fewkes believes these stones to have been
zemis or idols, and takes exception to the views of Mason,
Navarette and others that they represent volcanic agencies.
But he does so evidently without being aware of Maya
myths which, by analogy, greatly strengthen the supposi-
tions of these writers. I refer to the Maya conception of
the cosmos, which speaks of the earth as being supported

[1] "Estudios de arqueologia de Puerto Rico," article in *El Noticio*,
May, 1896. Reprinted in *Aquila*, Ponce, April and May, 1904, according
to Fewkes.

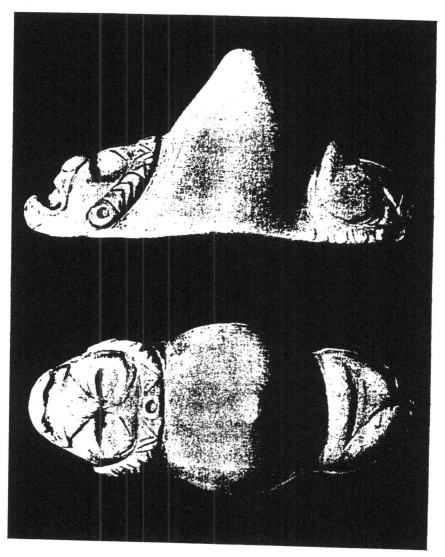

PLATE XVI.—THREE-POINTED STONES.
From the Antilles (after Fewkes).

on the back of a great dragon (the Gucumatz ?), four-footed whale, or other monster. Certain myths, too, in the Popol Vuh allude to gods known as Zipacna and Cabrakan, volcanic deities who heaped up the mountains and bore them on their backs. But, above all, we have the myth of Atlas itself, the story of the world-bearer, associated with Atlantis, and reflected in Quetzalcoatl, who is merely another form of Gucumatz, the dragon or serpent who dwelt in the sea. That these three-pointed stones refer to some such figure who can doubt ? They seem to me a reminiscence of a volcanic deity, a deity whose duty it was to uphold the earth, but who, on occasion, cast his burden from him, causing universal destruction and cataclysm.[1]

In these three-pointed stones, then, it seems to me we have Atlas represented in the shape of the symbolic pick as well as the world-bearer. In the thunder-stone seems to centre the whole significance of what I call the Atlantean culture-complex, which embraced the practice of mummification, witchcraft, the mysteries and the art of building in stone. It is the hub of a wheel of which they are the spokes. The flint or thunder-stone was the chisel of the Maya masons and sculptors, the magical implement that shaped the idol and the pyramid. The hammer of the thunder-god or the creative deity with which he carved and shaped the mountains and valleys was the selfsame implement as that with which the early sculptor carved the idol by what is known as " the crumbling process." The Algonquin Indian myths of Manibozho tell how he shaped the hills and dales with the hammer, constructing great beaver-dams and moles across the lakes—that " he carved the land and sea to his liking." Do we find any similar legend associated with Atlantis ? We do. Poseidon, we are told, carved the island of Atlantis into alternate zones of land and water. We are not informed with what implement he effected this. But, as he was indubitably a god of earthquake as well as a deity of the sea, it is a fair inference that he employed the thunder-stone or thunder-hammer, the shaping tool of the early mason, the great primeval pick, which consisted of a sharp flint beak set in a wooden haft, the hammer of Thor, the hammer of Ptah.

[1] See my essay on the Popol Vuh, 1908.

The operation of land-moulding in all mythologies is undertaken by the aid of this implement, and there is no reason to suppose that Atlantean myth differed from others in this respect.

The implement of the god is, of course, as sacred as the god himself, for the simple reason that it has absorbed his virtue. It is his fetish, his symbol, it comes in time to represent him, to act as his surrogate, so to speak. So, it would seem, was the case in Atlantis. The sacred flint pick-hammer of Poseidon became symbolic of him in the island-continent, it was probably kept wrapped up in linen, in his temple, as the black stone of Jupiter—the stone into which the god had been turned when an infant —was kept in his shrine at Pergamos, or the arrows of Uitzilopochtli in his teocalli at Mexico. A similar stone fetish is that enshrined in the Kaaba at Mecca, where it is wrapped up in silks. From Atlantis this idea of godhead may have spread to America on the one hand and to Spain and Europe generally on the other, eventually reaching localities so widely apart as Egypt and Scandinavia.

We find in the myths of the Toltecs of Mexico mention of a certain Huemac, or " Great Hand," associated with Quetzalcoatl, the culture-hero from the east, and perhaps identical with him, and in those of the Maya a Kab-ul, or " Working Hand." This is, of course, a deification of the hand which wields the craftsman's tool, as is obvious from its representations in the native manuscripts. Quetzalcoatl was the craftsman, the mason, the artificer cunning in the making of jewellery and beautiful things, who came out of the Atlantic. In his Maya-Quiche form of Tohil he is represented by a flint stone. Here, then, we have the culture-bringer who came out of the sea actually represented by what seems to be the central symbol and nucleus of the Atlantean culture-complex. Moreover, he is associated with the planet Venus. Indeed, he *is* that planet. We will remember that the interpreter of the Aztec Codex, Telleriano-Remensis, says of him : " They name him ' one Cane,' which is the star Venus, of which they tell the fable accredited among them. Tlauizcalpan Tecutli is the star Venus, the first created light before the deluge. *This star is Quetzalcoatl.*" This identification, of course, binds the various parts of the Atlantis complex together with double strength. Quetzalcoatl, it is also to be noted, "caused hurricanes" and "destroyed the world by wind," as the god of the flint stone well might have done.

But we find this Great Hand even more closely identified with Atlantis in the mediæval legends associated with the Atlantic Ocean. In the map of Bianco, dated 1436, is to be observed an island having the strange legend underneath it "Yd laman Satanaxio," generally translated "The Hand of Satan." Formaleoni, an Italian writer, noticed it, and failed to understand the allusion until he chanced quite fortuitously to stumble on a reference to a similar name in an old Italian romance, which told how, in a certain part of "India," a great hand rose every day from the sea and carried off a number of the inhabitants into the ocean. The tale is evidently eloquent of earthquake or similar catastrophe, of which it seems to be a memory. It seems pretty clear that the "Great Hand" was the deity of this Atlantic island, precisely as he was of the Mexicans and Maya, a god who took tribute of human lives by earthquake, and that some Atlantean memory of him must have drifted to Europe. In Central America maidens were sacrificed to Quetzalcoatl by drowning, and, as we have seen, the same procedure was followed in the Canary Islands, where the sacred virgins cast themselves into the sea as an offering to the god of ocean. The Maya were not resident on the coast, so it is clear that they must have retained the ceremony as a memorial of a period when they did live in an oceanic environment.

Quetzalcoatl was, moreover, the magician *par excellence*, and was especially worshipped by those tribes who practised mummification. He was also, we will recall, a twin as well as an earth-bearer, as was Atlas, and he it was who brought with him to Mexico from his Atlantic home the mysterious books which Nuñez de la Vega found at Huehuetenango in Soconusco in 1691. In Quetzalcoatl, then, centres every phase and aspect of the great Atlantean culture-complex.

In the account of Plato, brief as it is, most of the details of that complex will be found. In Central America and Mexico all of them centre in the figure of Quetzalcoatl. In Europe and Egypt their association with one figure is not so clearly revealed, which shows that the appearance of the complex in those regions must have taken place at a much earlier date, and when they were still in the stage of development. And, surely, if we find the whole circumstances of Plato's myth of Atlantis reproduced in America, we are justified in speaking of "Atlantis in America."

But in North Africa, on the other side of the Atlantic, the Atlas-Quetzalcoatl myth is practically reproduced in its entirety. We find there the twin-god and world-bearer (Atlas), his sacred mountain (the Atlas range), the art of mummification, witches or weird sorceresses in the Gorgons, the worship of flint stones or hammers as fetishes, the shaping of localities into land and water. Indeed, M. A. Rutot in his pamphlet *L'Atlantide*, published in Brussels in 1920, goes so far as to assume that Atlantis is identical with the regions now known as Morocco, Algeria and Tunis, which about 1200 B.C., he says, were cut off from the mainland of Africa by an earthquake. This caused a subsidence and flooded what is now the chain of lakes between the Gulf of Kabes on the east and the Wady Draa on the west. It thus became isolated from the rest of the civilised world for a prolonged period.

This and similar theories seem to me to fall to the ground when the extraordinary corroboration of the American evidence is kept in view. Is it possible for circumstances to be more positively paralleled than those of the Atlantic-American tradition in the west and the Atlantic-Euro-African tradition in the east?

Finally, does not this complex with all its distinctive associations show a clearly defined bond of connection from Egypt to Mexico? Do not the traditions of the sunken continent cluster more vividly round the coastal fringes of Western Europe and Eastern America than elsewhere in these areas? Are not the advanced island-groups of these two continents replete with proofs of their former occupation by this complex? If these things are not so, my contention is futile. But as they are certainly so, that contention deserves rational consideration.

I might easily have laboured my advocacy of these arguments in a much longer treatise than the present. This might have lent it greater weight, for undue compression is often fatal to demonstration. But I trust to the very clear, obvious and striking nature of the facts and proofs, the illustrations and resemblances I have brought together in these pages to convince my readers of the soundness of my theory that Atlantean civilisation reached America rather than to the implications or prolixities of argument which are so frequently encountered when the justification of a hypothesis is attempted.

CHRONOLOGICAL TABLE

Crô-Magnon race, or first Atlantean wave, arrives
in Europe at close of the Ice Age, about . . 23,000 B.C.

Magdalenian race, or second Atlantean wave,
arrives in Europe, about . . . . 14,000 ,,

Azilian-Tardenoisian race, or third Atlantean
wave, arrives in Europe, about . . . 10,000 ,,

Final submergence of Atlantis, according to
Plato . . . . 9,600 ,,

Antillia partly or finally submerged, and arrival
of the Maya, an Antillian race, in America,
about. . . . . 200 ,,

Desertion of the cities of Guatemala by the Maya,
and settlement of the Maya-Toltec in Mexico
and Yucatan, about . . . . . 600 A.D.

Note.—There is a consensus of opinion as regards all of these
dates excepting that given by Plato, which it is naturally
impossible to verify absolutely. At the same time, the arrival
of the Azilian-Tardenoisians in Europe approximately at that
period seems to support the strong likelihood of contemporary
submergence in the Atlantic area, especially as the region of
their origin has not as yet been agreed upon by archæologists.
The same remark applies to the entrance into Europe of the
Crô-Magnon and Magdalenian waves of immigration, which
probably took place subsequent to profound seismic disturbances or partial submergence in the Atlantic. A similar deduction may be arrived at in the case of the submergence of
Antillia, the date of which is unknown, but may be inferred
from the sudden appearance of the Maya in Central America
from a region unknown. These conclusions are also substantiated by the proved analogy of arrivals in Easter Island
from a submerged locality.

INDEX

Abercromby, Lord, quoted, 16 ; on the Guanches, 38

Acosta, quoted, 126

Al-tin, supposed Arabic name of Antillia, 19

Amazons, 129–31 ; suggested etymology of the name, 131 ; of Mexico, 132 ; sacred axe of the, 140

Ameghino, his theories of man's antiquity in America, 135–6

America, invasion of by Atlantean-Antillian race, 40 ; traditions of Atlantis in, 65–80 ; myth of compared with Atlantean myth, 77 ; bull sacrifice in, 96 ; mummification in, 99–122 ; antiquity of man in, 134–40 ; European influence in, 139–40 ; Asiatic influence in, 140–1 ; Polynesian influence in, 141–4 ; routes of migration to, 144 ; immigration from Atlantis to, 144–5 ; pyramids of, 157–65 ; mounds in, 161–4 ; traditions of white men in, 174–6

American religion, Atlantean tradition in, 81–98 ; ritual connection between and those of Europe and North Africa, 91–2

Antillean archipelago, a fragment of Atlantis, 17

Antillean continent, Spencer on geology of, 26 ; Scharff on, 27 ; Böse on, 27 ; summary of geological evidence on, 27–9 ; terrestrial and cultural relations with Atlantis, 30–4, 33–40 ; Crô-Magnons enter, 40

Antilles, as remains of ancient continent of Antillia, 20–9 ; Suess on geology of, 21 ; Scharff on, 21–2 ; Hill on, 22 ; Schuchert on, 22–6 ; Simpson on, 22 ; fauna of the, 22–7 ; Gadow on, 25 ; Ortmann on, 25 ; pyramids in, 158–9 ; Maya in, 194 ; insects of, 25 ; birds of, 25 ; seismic disturbances in, 57 ; pyramids in, 158–9 ; the Maya race in, 194 ; three-pointed stones of the, 197–200

Antillia, confused with West Indian Islands, 18 ; traditions referring to, 18–21 ; in Cancrio's map, 19 ; in Egerton MS. maps, 19 ; supposed to be one with Atlantis, 19 ; supposed Arabic name of,

19 ; maps of, antedating discovery of America, 20 ; identified with Cuba, 20–9

Architecture, evidence from, 155–65

Aristotle, on the Atlantic, 190

Art, evidence from, 149–55

Asia, error of searching for all American origins in, 97–8, 110 ; mummification not introduced into America from, 120

Asiatic influences in American culture, 140–1

Atlantean theory, modern protagonists of, 15 ; culture, route of its introduction into America, 17

Atlantic, Admiralty soundings in the, 33, 192 ; great ridge of the, 33

Atlantis, Plato's account of, 14–15 ; existence of man on, 16 ; former conclusions upon, 17 ; disintegration of, 17 ; former existence of, 30–4 ; Termier on, 30–1 ; Scharff on, 31 ; biology of, 32 ; maritime shores as remains of, 32 ; probable date of final submergence of, 33 ; Crô-Magnon race as emigrants from, 34–40 ; myths relating to in America, 65–80 ; account of in Plato's Critias, 65 ; myth of compared with American traditions, 77 ; traditions of in American religions, 81–98 ; bull sacrifice in, 94 ; witchcraft in, 129–33 ; elephant a native of, 152 ; sacred hill of, 157–61 ; tradition of Lemuria compared with that of, 176–85 ; resemblance of the ruins of Metalanim to, 183 ; Maya a race from, 194–6 ; culture-complex of, 200–2 ; Rutot on, 202

Atlas, myth of, 77–8 ; three-pointed stones associated with, 199–202

Aurignacian culture, 36 ; Breuil on, 36 ; theory of African origin of, 36 ; new phase of, 38 ; invasion of America by, 40–1 ; germs of mummification in, 99–100 ; Maya art-forms developed from, 149 ; art, 149–55 ; hand-stencilling, 150–1 ; resemblance of to American-Indian art, 151 ; use of shell ornaments, 154–5

Avienus, on the Atlantic, 190

O

Lightning Source UK Ltd.
Milton Keynes UK
UKHW041818061122
411751UK00001B/21